Donna Dewberry's
ALL NEW book of
one-stroke
painting

Donna Dewberry's
ALL NEW book of
one-stroke
painting

NORTH LIGHT BOOKS
CINCINNATI, OHIO
www.artistsnetwork.com

Published by North Light Books, an imprint of F+W Publications, Inc., 4700 E. Galbraith Rd., Cincinnati, Ohio, 45236. (800) 289-0963. First edition.

Other fine North Light Books are available from your local bookstore, art supply store or direct from the publisher.

10 09 08 07   6 5 4 3

Distributed in Canada by Fraser Direct
100 Armstrong Avenue
Georgetown, ON, Canada L7G 5S4
Tel: (905) 877-4411

Distributed in the U.K. and Europe by David & Charles
Brunel House, Newton Abbot, Devon, TQ12 4PU, England
Tel: (+44) 1626 323200, Fax: (+44) 1626 323319
Email: mail@davidandcharles.co.uk

Distributed in Australia by Capricorn Link
P.O. Box 704, S. Windsor NSW, 2756 Australia
Tel: (02) 4577-3555

Library of Congress Cataloging-in-Publication Data

Dewberry, Donna S.
   Donna Dewberry's all new book of one-stroke painting / Donna Dewberry.—1st ed.
      p. cm.
   Includes index.
   ISBN-13: 978-1-58180-705-9 (hbk. : alk. paper)
   ISBN-10: 1-58180-705-8 (hbk. : alk. paper)

   ISBN-13: 978-1-58180-706-6 (pbk. : alk. paper)
   ISBN-10: 1-58180-706-6 (pbk. : alk. paper)
   1. Painting. 2. Decoration and ornament. I. Title.
   TT385.D477 2005
   745.7'23—dc22
                                          2005013759

Editor: Kathy Kipp
Production Coordinator: Kristen Heller
Cover Designer: Clare Finney
Designers: Clare Finney and Amy F. Wilkin/Dragonfly Graphics, L.L.C.
Layout Artist: Amy F. Wilkin/Dragonfly Graphics, L.L.C.
Photographers: Christine Polomsky and Al Parrish

about the author

Donna Dewberry began her career in crafting and decorating at a young age. Her mother and grandmother taught her how to sew her own clothing for school. This love for creating beautiful things expanded into her married life as she began decorating her own home and the homes of her friends. She started by making draperies and painting murals on walls. In 1995 with the help of Plaid Enterprises, the One-Stroke technique came to life. Donna is a native Floridian and has been married for over 30 years. She has seven children and seven grandchildren. This is her eighth book for North Light on the One-Stroke painting technique.

metric conversion chart

To convert	to	multiply by
Inches	Centimeters	2.54
Centimeters	Inches	0.4
Feet	Centimeters	30.5
Centimeters	Feet	0.03
Yards	Meters	0.9
Meters	Yards	1.1
Sq. Inches	Sq. Centimeters	6.45
Sq. Centimeters	Sq. Inches	0.16
Sq. Feet	Sq. Meters	0.09
Sq. Meters	Sq. Feet	10.8
Sq. Yards	Sq. Meters	0.8
Sq. Meters	Sq. Yards	1.2
Pounds	Kilograms	0.45
Kilograms	Pounds	2.2
Ounces	Grams	28.3
Grams	Ounces	0.035

a note from Donna

*I*t is so important to find a hobby or craft that we love to do and that keeps us busy. Finding our passion and developing our talents bring so much joy and confidence to our lives. One-Stroke painting is my passion; I love being able to create and share new and innovative ideas with the use of the One-Stroke technique. God has blessed my life in so many ways; one is being given the opportunity to share One-Stroke painting with many people throughout the world. I have also been blessed to work with many talented painters as well as other artists in their respective fields who are professional, caring, and passionate about what they do. Each of these people has touched and enriched my life. Meeting them has expanded my circle of friends and for that I am ever so grateful. Like the One-Stroke technique that has evolved in so many different ways, I look forward to the future as the One-Stroke family continues to grow.

—Donna Dewberry

dedication

I would like to dedicate this book to a person who has understood my vision, passion, and excitement from the beginning. She has always seen a wonderful future in One-Stroke painting and brings her own creative flair to every aspect of the technique. She consistently gives me inspiration for new Donna Dewberry One-Stroke books published by North Light. Thank you, Kathy Kipp, for all your support, patience, and dedication as well as for being my editor and friend. You are incredible!

what is "one-stroke" painting?

A fast and easy technique in which the brush is loaded with two or more colors so you can blend, shade and highlight all in one stroke of the brush.

table of contents

Beyond One-Stroke

Donna's Tips for Great Design

12 Step-by-Step Projects

materials

brushes

flat brushes

Painting the One-Stroke technique requires the use of flat brushes. All the projects in this book were painted with the Donna Dewberry One Stroke brushes made by Plaid. These brushes are specially designed with longer bristles and less thickness in the brush body to allow for a much sharper chisel edge. A sharp chisel edge is essential to the success of the One-Stroke technique, since most strokes start and end on the chisel edge of the brush. (Refer to "Parts of the Brush" on page 16 to see the chisel edge of the brush.) Flat brushes come in all sizes, but the ones I use most often are the ¾-inch (19mm) and the no. 12. They hold a lot of paint yet still maintain their sharp chisel edge.

angular brushes

Angular brushes are flats that have bristles cut at an angle: the "toe" is the longer side and the "heel" is the shorter side. Angular brushes can make it easier to paint such things as comma strokes and vines. The One Stroke angular brushes come in ⅜-inch (10mm), ⅝-inch (16mm) and ¾-inch (19mm) sizes.

scruffy brushes

The scruffy brush I created for the One-Stroke technique has many uses and makes it easy and fun to paint things like moss, wisteria, lilacs, some hair and fur, faux finishes and shading textures. Before using this brush for the first time, be sure to "fluff the scruff." Remove the brush from the package and form the natural hair bristles into an oval shape by gently pulling on them. Then twist the bristles in your palm until you have an oval shape. When fluffed, the scruffy is ready to use for painting.

Do not wet this brush prior to loading it with paint. If you need to clean paint color out of a scruffy, rinse it with water and dry the bristles well on a paper towel before reloading it with paint. To clean the scruffy, pounce the bristles into a brush basin of water. Do not rake them across the bottom or you will break the natural hair bristles.

script liners

For the One-Stroke painting technique, I use two sizes of script liners. Liners are thin round brushes with long bristles that hold a lot of paint. The no. 1 script liner is usually used for small detail work where more control is needed. The no. 2 script liner is used where a bit less control is needed, such as for loosely flowing curlicues and tendrils.

In One-Stroke painting, the liner brush is always used with paint that has been thinned to an "inky" consistency. To achieve this consistency, pour a small amount of paint onto your palette. Dip the liner brush into clean water, then touch the water to your palette, next to

BRUSHES
1–3 Lettering brushes. **4–12** Enamels brushes for glass and ceramics; shown are two liners, three flats, an angular brush, a filbert, and a small and large scruffy. **13–17** In this row are brushes for use with acrylics, starting with five sizes of flats. **18–20** Three sizes of scruffies. **21–22** Two sizes of script liners. **23–24** Two sizes of angular brushes. **25** This is a round faux finish sponge with a built-in handle to keep paint off your hands. **26** Two shapes of sponge painters.

the paint puddle. Do this three or four times. Use a circular motion to mix the water with the edge of the paint puddle until you have an inky consistency. Don't mix all of the paint with the water or your mixture will be too thick. Roll the brush handle between your fingers as you pull out of the inky paint—this will sharpen the tip of the brush and prevent the paint from dripping. (See page 19 for instructions on how to load a liner brush.)

Clean these brushes by rinsing them in a brush basin filled with clean water. Be gentle, but clean them thoroughly.

enamels brushes for glass and ceramics

These brushes are made specifically for painting on smooth surfaces such as glass and ceramics. They have very soft bristles to minimize brushstrokes, but the bristles still spring back to a chisel edge, which is essential to One-Stroke painting.

lettering brushes

This set of brushes includes two flats and one script liner. The two flat brushes have contour handles that keep the brush at the optimum 45-degree angle perfect for calligraphy style lettering.

sponges
faux finish sponge

Perfectly formed to fit in the hand, the round shape and rounded edges of this sponge help to create a perfect faux effect without any hard edges.

sponge painters

Available in four shapes and sizes, these feature two different textures to maintain clean painted edges while minimizing paint bleeding onto the hand.

enamels detail painters

These sponges are essential for making perfect berries and grapes. They can even be double- and multi-loaded.

paints
acrylics

For all the projects in this book, I used Plaid FolkArt Acrylic paints and mediums available from any arts and crafts supply store. FolkArt acrylics are high quality paints that come in 2-oz. (59ml) plastic bottles in a wide array of premixed colors. There are so many colors available that you will seldom need to mix colors to get just the right one. Some of the most-used colors also come in larger economical 8-oz. (236ml) bottles. Their

rich and creamy formulation and long open time make them perfect for decorative painting and home decor projects.

Acrylic paints are convenient and fun to use. They are odorless and water-based so there are no solvents needed. Cleanup is easy—just use water to rinse the paint out of your brushes while you're working, then use a gentle brush cleaning gel to clean and condition your brushes at the end of the day.

You'll find many brands of acrylics at your local craft store, but you can avoid frustration and disappointment by always buying the best quality materials you can afford—it will make your painting experience much more rewarding. If you can't find the colors you need at your local stores, see the Resources section in the back of the book for other sources.

artists' pigments

FolkArt Artists' Pigments also come in handy 2-oz. (59ml) plastic bottles but they have a higher pigment concentration than regular acrylic paints so they're able to create a more intense coverage. Their deep, true colors blend easily and maintain their vibrancy when mixed. Because Artists' Pigments are acrylics, they're easy to clean up.

PAINTS AND MEDIUMS

1 Enamels, for painting on glass, china, tiles, metal and other hard, nonporous surfaces. **2** Papier Paint for paper and wood. **3** Outdoor Paints resist UV rays and weather. **4** Acrylics, Artists' Pigments and Metallics are perfect for surfaces ranging from wood to walls. **5** Mediums are formulated to work with specific types of paint.

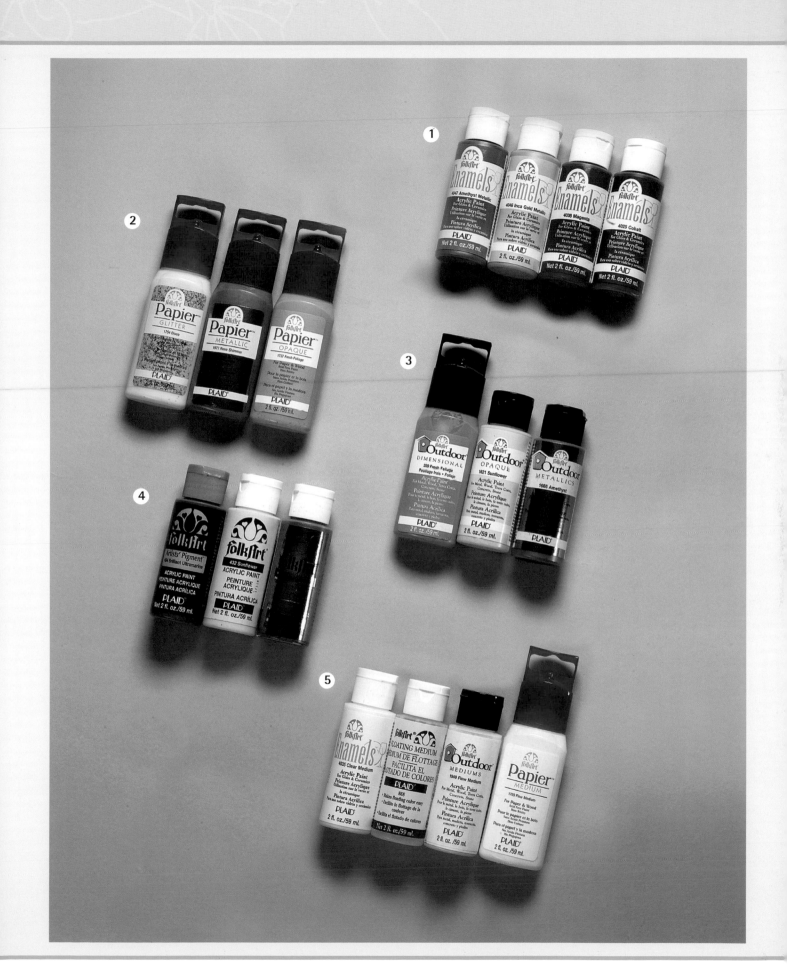

metallic paints

These gleaming metallic paints add a beautiful shine to your projects. They are highly pigmented, but since they are water-based acrylics, they can be easily cleaned up with soap and water.

enamels

FolkArt Enamels are specially formulated to stick to hard, nonporous surfaces such as glass, china, ceramics, mirrors, and metal. They can be baked in your household oven or air cured for 21 days. They are dishwasher safe but you may want to hand-wash your painted pieces anyway. Never use water to thin Enamels; instead use FolkArt Clear Medium the same way you would use Floating Medium or water with regular acrylic paints.

All of the painting on a surface needs to be done within the same 24 hour period. If more elements are added after the initial 24 hours have passed, then make sure the new paint is not overlapping existing paint.

If you are painting elements that have overlapping layers, such as a rose, paint quickly so that wet paint is going on top of wet paint. If the lower layer of paint is in a partially dry stage and you apply another stroke on top, the lower layer of paint can lift up in places, causing a blotchy effect. If you are not a fast painter, then use a blow dryer or heat gun and dry the paint to the touch before painting a top layer.

papier paints

Papier Opaques are specially made for painting on porous surfaces such as paper and wood. They contain very little water to minimize the warping of paper, and they are acid free and archivally safe. All Papier paints are bottled in writer-tip bottles, which means they can be used straight from the bottle to outline, embellish or write. When using the paint this way, always pull the bottle rather than pushing it. Try to keep an even pressure on the bottle and keep moving at an even pace. To stop a line, release the pressure prior to lifting.

Papier paints can also be used with a brush. FolkArt's brushes for paper surfaces are made especially for use with this paint, with stiffer bristles to move the paint. Papier Flow Medium is also needed when using brushes.

Papier Metallic paint is highly pigmented with finely ground metallic dust. Papier Glitter paint contains coarser metallic particles. Both of these will add shimmer and dazzle to your projects. Papier Glass Effects paint adds yet another dimension. Make cherries glisten with ripeness or add to painted water to create a reflective surface.

outdoor paints

These can be used on painted or unpainted metal, tin, terra cotta, wood, stone and concrete. They have a sealer in them to resist UV rays and weather conditions. Outdoor paints come in opaques, metallics and dimensionals.

mediums
how to use mediums

The mediums I use are specific to the type of paint they are made for. You cannot use a medium designed for Papier paints with Enamels or Acrylics and vice versa. Just because each type of paint has a medium called "Flow Medium" does not mean that they are same thing. Each medium has a chemical make-up specifically formulated for a certain type of paint.

floating medium

Floating Medium is a clear gel that allows your acrylic paints to stay wetter, which helps make your brush strokes smoother and more continuous without dry spots or breaks. It's very easy to use—just load your brush with paint, then dip the tip of the bristles straight down into a puddle of floating medium on your palette. Stroke back and forth two or three times on your palette to work the medium into the bristles. Now you're ready to paint. Do not pick up floating medium every time you pick up paint; it needs to be added only if your strokes start to drag or feel dry.

clear medium

This is the medium for Enamels. It is used the same way that Floating Medium is used with Acrylics. It helps extend the stroke and avoid "dry" edges. I use it by dipping a fully loaded brush into it and blending into the brush. It can also be used to make "shadow" effects.

flow medium

Also known as "Donna's curlicue medium," this medium will thin Enamels paints to an ink-like consistency without degrading the durability of the paint like water will.

papier flow medium

This is the medium to use with Papier paints. It is needed when using a brush. You will need to pick up Papier Flow Medium as you are loading the brush with paint. Papier paint is extremely thick and Flow Medium is used to make the paint more manageable.

outdoor flow medium

This is the medium for Outdoor Paints. It is used in the same manner as Floating Medium for Acrylics. It helps extend the stroke and avoid "dry" edges. I use it by dipping a fully loaded brush into it and blending it into the brush. It can also be used to make "shadow" effects.

other supplies

palette

The FolkArt One Stroke Palette I use is durable, handy, lightweight and comfortable to hold. The green plastic palette has numerous paint wells around the rim for all your colors plus some floating medium. There are also holes of different sizes to hold your brushes upright while you paint, and a large hole for your thumb and a folded paper towel. The palette is designed for either right- or left-handed use.

The center holds a 9-inch (23cm) disposable foam plate. These Styrofoam plates are perfect for working with the water-based acrylic paints I use, and I can buy them in bulk at the grocery or discount store. I use the foam plate to place my colors on, to load my brushes with paint, and to stroke back and forth to work the paint into the bristles. I keep some floating medium in one of the wells so that it's handy to dip into whenever I need it. There are tabs on the palette to hold the foam plate in place while you paint. When you're finished, just lift the plate out of the palette and throw it away.

brush caddy

The FolkArt One Stroke brush caddy is what I use to hold water for my brushes, to clean my brushes, and to keep them upright when not in use. The caddy has two sides: one side has a large cleaning rake along the bottom and the other side has a divided resting area to keep the brushes in the water but off of their bristles. To clean your flats and angular brushes, fill the larger side with clean water and rake the bristles along the ribbed bottom a few times to work the paint out of brush. Be sure to clean the paint out of the ferrule too. (See "Parts of the Brush" on page 16).

After cleaning, the brush can be stored in one of the holes along the rim. If your brush is still loaded with paint, you can slip it into one of the notches on the other rim to keep it up off your table until you need it again.

The brush caddy comes with a ventilated lid with a handle for easy and safe carrying. The smooth plastic makes it easy to rinse out dirty, painty water and fill again with clean water.

brush cleaner and conditioner

This is a bottled gel that is strong enough to remove paint from bristles but gentle to your hands and your brushes.

brush preserver

This is a round plastic disk with nibs of four different heights to scrub all sizes of your brushes clean. Use with the Brush Cleaner and Conditioner to help preserve your brushes.

tracing paper and transfer paper

You'll need plain white tracing paper to trace the patterns for the projects in this book. Place the tracing paper over the pattern and use a pencil or ballpoint pen to trace the pattern lines.

Transfer paper, or graphite paper, is used to transfer the lines of the pattern onto the surface. See page 57 for step-by-step instructions on transferring a pattern.

paint eraser tool set

Eraser tools are perfect for wiping away wet paint off a smooth surface to clean up the edges and fix errant brushstrokes. The set includes three tools with flat chisel-edge tips and one pointed round tool.

tip-pen craft tips

These tips come in a set of three metal tips of different sizes and two plastic bottle caps. You can attach these tips to bottles of Enamels or Papier paints to make fine lines of dimensional paint on your surface. They can also be used with any FolkArt acrylic paint to make fine lines.

acrylic lacquer

FolkArt Lacquer comes in three finishes: matte, satin and gloss. These fast-drying spray-on lacquers are formulated to use indoors or out. They leave a smooth, clear, even finish and diminish naturally occurring imperfections in wood. Use them on wooden and metal surfaces.

SUPPLIES
1 White transfer paper. **2** Paint Eraser tool set. **3** One Stroke Palette with a foam plate in the center. **4** FolkArt acrylic spray lacquer. **5** Tip-Pen Craft Tips. **6** Brush Cleaner and Conditioner, and a Brush Preserver. **7** Black transfer paper. **8** FolkArt brush caddy (lid not shown). **9** Enamels Detail Painters with sponge tips.

getting started

parts of the brush

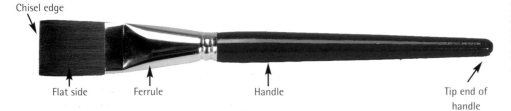

Chisel edge

Flat side   Ferrule   Handle   Tip end of handle

about the flat brush

This is a 1-inch (25mm) flat brush made especially for One-Stroke painting. The tips of the bristles are called the "chisel edge," or "chisel" for short. When you are painting, you need to start the stroke on the chisel edge and finish the stroke on the chisel edge. This means you should not be applying any pressure on the bristles.

In this book, I will often say "lay the flat side of the bristles down" or "lean on the chisel edge." The "flat" side of the bristles is shown above; laying the flat side of the bristles down means to apply pressure in the direction of the flat part. Whereas, "lean on the chisel edge" means to lean in the direction of the thin sides.

I use flat brushes most of the time rather than other shapes because I can achieve many different kinds of strokes with just one brush. By stroking in the direction of the chisel edge and tilting the brush handle back a little and lifting the leading edge off of the surface slightly, I can paint thin vines and grass very quickly. But by keeping the handle of the brush straight up and down and applying pressure in the direction of the chisel edge to lean the bristles in that direction, I can paint thick branches or daisy petals.

Moving the brush in different directions and experimenting with varying amounts of pressure makes the possibilities nearly endless as to what you can do with a flat brush. This is one of the reasons that One-Stroke painting is so quick and easy. People are always amazed at how fast I can paint a design. Part of the reason is how I load my brush; the other is using only one brush to paint many things.

parts of the angular brush

HEEL
On an angular brush, the heel is the shorter side of the bristles.

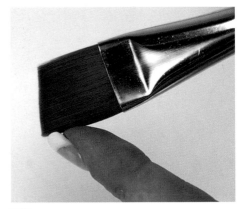

TOE
The toe is the longer side of the bristles. Hold the brush so the toe is at the top.

how to load the brush

double loading a flat brush

1 A properly loaded brush is essential to being able to paint using the One-Stroke technique. If your brush is not properly loaded, you will not have enough paint to finish the stroke. A properly loaded brush should feel like you are painting with soft butter.

First, moisten the brush with water, then blot off on a paper towel. Dip one corner of the flat brush into the first color. Turn the brush over and dip the other corner into the second color.

2 Work the paint into the bristles by stroking back and forth in a track on the palette. Try to keep this track no more than 2 inches (5cm) long. Any longer than that and you are taking paint off of the brush instead of working it into the brush. Push hard initially to work the paint up into the bristles. Keep picking up paint and working it into the brush until it is about three-fourths of the way up toward the ferrule. Make sure that the handle of the brush is straight up and down. If you tilt to the left or the right you will cause the paint to become overmixed and muddy looking. Notice how my track is in between the puddles of paint and the darker side of my brush is on the same side as the darker puddle of paint? This prevents picking up new color on the wrong side of the brush.

multi-loading a flat brush

1 To multi-load your brush with more than two colors, dip one corner of a double-loaded brush into a third color. In this photo, I loaded yellow onto the white corner. Generally, we will always load a lighter color onto the lightest corner of the brush.

2 Work the paint into the bristles by stroking the brush back and forth in the same track on the palette. Try not to extend your track any longer than it was during your double loading.

double loading a scruffy brush

2 See how only one-half of the bristles are loaded with paint?

4 Now you can see how the brush is double-loaded evenly with the two colors.

1 A scruffy is loaded differently than a flat brush. Never dip a scruffy into the middle of the paint puddle. Instead, pounce the scruffy at the edge of the puddle to load half of the brush with your first color.

3 Now pounce the other side of the scruffy into the edge of the puddle of the darker color.

multi-loading a scruffy brush

1 Pounce the light side of the double-loaded scruffy brush into the edge of a puddle of another lighter color. Here I'm loading the white side into yellow.

2 Pounce the dark side of the scruffy into the edge of a puddle of another dark color. Here, the green side is being loaded into brown.

3 Check your bristles—if your scruffy is properly loaded, you should be able to clearly see all four colors.

loading a script liner with inky paint

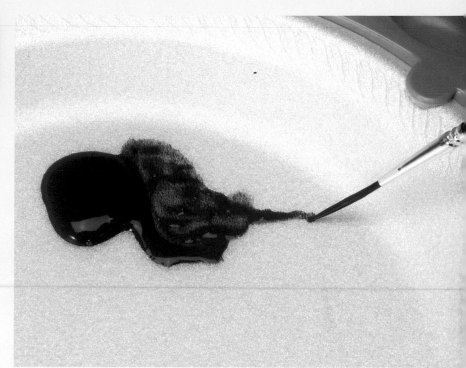

1 Dip the script liner into some water and let the water drop onto the palette next to the puddle of paint. Move the brush in a circular motion pulling a little paint into the water to thin the paint to an inky consistency. It might be necessary to add more water two or three times.

2 As you pull the brush out, roll the brush in your fingers and drag the tip of the brush on the palette to bring the bristles to a point.

loading the brush handle end

2 Touch the handle end to the center area of the flower and lift straight out. Don't turn or twist the handle or make a circular motion.

1 This is the easiest way to dot in the centers of flowers. Turn your brush upside down and dip the tip end of the handle into the paint, holding your brush straight up and down.

side-loading a flat brush

1 Load the first color onto both sides of the flat.

2 Stroke next to the second color, allowing the bristles on one corner to touch the puddle of paint.

3 This is what a properly side-loaded brush looks like.

using floating medium

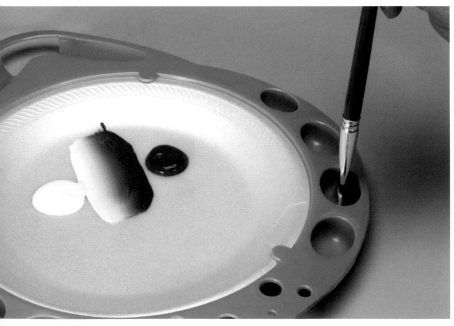

1 If you are going to be painting on a "dry" surface such as a wall or wood, then you will need to add Floating Medium. I like to keep the Floating Medium in one of the wells on my palette. When your brush is fully loaded with paint, dip the chisel edge of the loaded brush into the well of Floating Medium on your palette.

2 Work it into the bristles just like you did the paint, using the same track that you used to load the brush.

loading a sponge with paint

1 Dampen a round faux finish sponge with clean water first before picking up any paint. Wring it out well; you want the sponge to feel slightly damp, not wet. Load the sponge by moving it in a circular motion on your palette, pulling paint from the edge of the puddle.

2 A sponge can be double loaded just as a brush can. To double load, work the edge of the loaded side of the sponge into a second color, using a back-and-forth motion like an arc.

4 To load a rectangular sponge or any shape sponge that has a defined edge, use a back-and-forth motion to work the paint into the sponge from the edge of the paint puddle.

3 This is what a properly double-loaded sponge looks like.

5 See how just the very edge is loaded? This edge allows you paint fine lines on such things as a faux column or wall sconce (see page 146).

loading a sponge-end detail painter

1 This is a quick and easy way to paint blueberries, raspberries and grapes. Load the sponge end of the dabber by tapping it straight up and down at the edge of the puddle of your first color. Check the sponge end to be sure it's loaded correctly.

2 To load your second color, touch the loaded sponge end next to the edge of the puddle of paint and turn the dabber in your fingers back and forth to load the color around the outside edge of half of the sponge.

3 Place the loaded dabber on your surface and twist it back and forth in your fingers to create each berry. If you want a cluster, just overlap the berries as shown. Keep the lighter side on the same side of each berry. Do you see how each berry is highlighted and shaded in one motion?

proper brush handling

using a scruffy brush

1 When using a double-loaded scruffy brush to paint wisteria, moss, lilacs, etc., pounce the scruffy by holding the brush handle straight up and down.

2 To taper the ends of wisteria blossoms, lean the scruffy to the side so only one edge of it touches the surface, but still pounce straight up and down not sideways.

using a flat brush

1 To stay up on the chisel edge of the bristles, the brush handle must be straight up and down. You will start and end every stroke on the chisel.

2 When painting in the direction of the chisel edge, the color that follows will be the dominant color. Leaning the bristles in this direction and moving in the direction of the blue will result in the white being dominant at the beginning of the stroke. When leading with the darker color, you will need to pick up the lighter color more often. This is due to the lighter color constantly stroking over top of the darker color, mixing the darker color into the lighter color.

3 Most of the time I will lead with the lighter color, which keeps the colors fresh longer. For vines, grass, and most stems, I will use very little pressure. I even lift the leading edge slightly. For daisy petals, mums, and rosebud stems, I use more pressure to make the strokes fuller.

4 To start a shell stroke or a wiggle leaf, apply enough pressure so the flat side of the brush bends almost all the way up to the ferrule.

using an angular brush

2 Lean the brush to one side as you push down and slide the brush toward you.

1 Angular brushes make painting a ribbon very easy. Start by loading your dominant color on the toe (the longer side) of the angle brush and your secondary or highlight color on the heel (the shorter side). Start up on the chisel edge. The handle of this brush needs to tilt slightly, allowing the whole chisel edge to rest on the surface.

3 Lift back up to the chisel edge as you change direction, but don't stop moving.

4 Lean the brush to the opposite side as you push down and continue to slide the brush toward you.

5 Lift back up to the chisel edge to finish.

brush care and cleaning

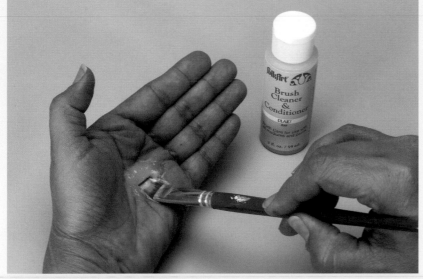

1 Place a dab of Brush Cleaner and Conditioner in the palm of your hand and work the brush back and forth in the cleaner to get the paint out of the bristles. Then rinse the brush in clean water.

2 If you would rather not use your hand, Plaid makes a small plastic Brush Preserver to use with the Cleaner/Conditioner. Place a dab of cleaner on your brush and work the bristles into whichever level of nubs is right for your size of brush—the bigger the brush, the longer the nubs. Rinse in clean water.

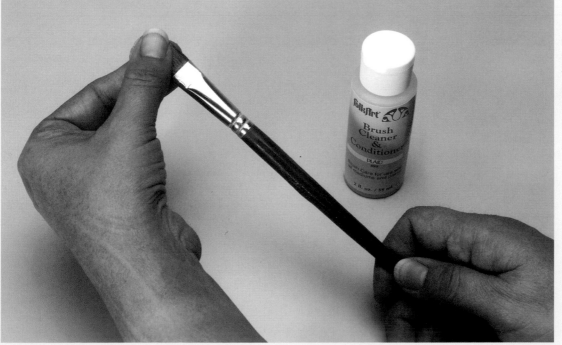

3 You can also use the Brush Cleaner and Conditioner to re-shape the bristles before storing your brush. Always dry the brush either laying flat or hanging with the bristles pointed down.

one-stroke painting techniques

basic strokes

chisel-edge stroke

1 Touch the chisel edge of the brush to the surface.

2 Lean the bristles in the direction of the stroke.

3 Pull the stroke at the same time as you lift back up to the chisel edge to finish the stroke.

REMEMBER...
The chisel edge of the brush is the very edge of the bristles on a flat or angular brush. A sharp chisel edge is essential to the One-Stroke painting technique, as many strokes start and end on the chisel edge.

c-stroke

1 Touch the chisel edge to the surface to make two parallel guidelines to mark the start and finish of the C-stroke.

2 Start on the chisel edge on the upper guideline.

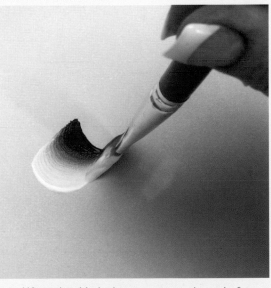

4 Lift to the chisel edge as you near the end of the stroke.

3 Lean the brush to the left as you put pressure on the bristles and start moving the brush in the shape of the letter C. Do not turn the brush during this stroke.

u-stroke

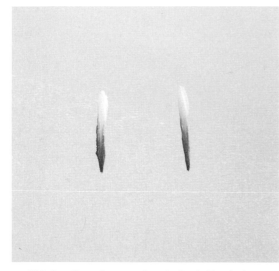

1 This is a C-stroke turned on its back. Touch the chisel edge to the surface to make two parallel guidelines to mark the start and finish of the U-stroke.

2 Start on the chisel edge on the left guideline.

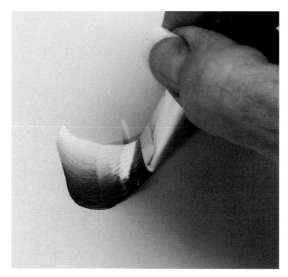

3 Lean the brush as you put pressure on the bristles and start forming the curve of the letter U.

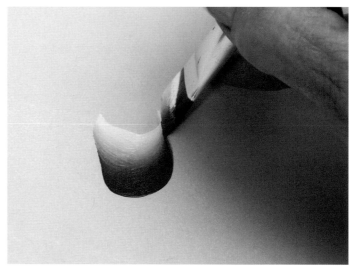

4 Finish the curve on the right guideline, lifting up to the chisel to end the stroke.

teardrop stroke

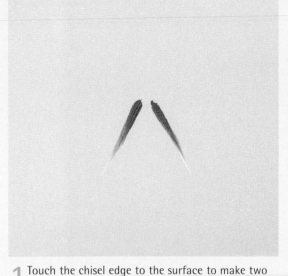

1 Touch the chisel edge to the surface to make two guidelines in an inverted V-shape.

2 Touch the chisel edge to one of the guidelines.

3 Stroke down and over to form a teardrop shape. Do not turn or twist the whole brush; only the bristles on the outer edge turn slightly.

4 Finish on the chisel edge of the brush at the point or base of the teardrop stroke.

one-stroke leaf & sunflower petal

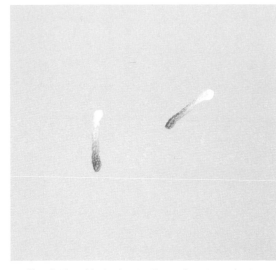

1 Touch the chisel edge to the surface to make two guidelines to mark the start and finish of the stroke. Place one pointing at 12 o'clock and the other pointing at about 1:30.

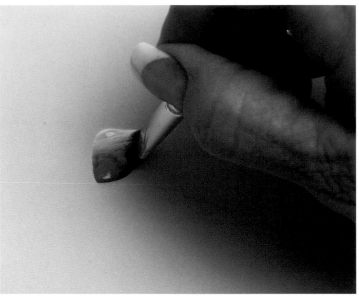

2 Start on the 12 o'clock guideline and push down on the bristles.

3 Turn the brush slightly to about the 1:30 guideline.

4 Slide forward as you lift back up to the chisel to finish the stroke on the other guideline.

shell stroke

1 Touch the chisel edge to the surface to make two guidelines in a V-shape. Leave the bottom of the V open.

2 Starting on the left guideline, press down on the bristles and make three starter strokes one on top of the other in the same place. These starter strokes help you feel the pressure and the rhythm of the stroke.

3 Press down on the bristles and wiggle the brush out and in as you turn in a fan-shape direction, pivoting on the lower side (in this case, the darker pink side) of the brush.

5 Slide back on the chisel edge slightly toward the base of the shell to finish the stroke.

4 As you reach the guideline on the right, lift back up to the chisel edge.

iris or tulip petal stroke

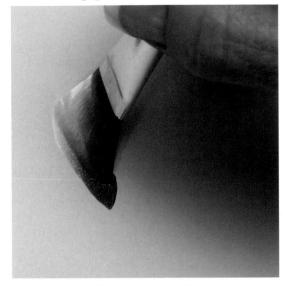

1 Start on the chisel edge and push down on the bristles.

2 Wiggle the brush and turn it slightly to the tip of the petal. Lift all the way up to the chisel at the tip of the petal to make it pointed.

3 Reverse direction of the bristles without lifting them from the surface. Compare the position of the bristles here with their position in Step 2.

4 Slide smoothly back to the base, lifting to the chisel edge to finish the stroke.

one-stroke flowers

daisies and asters

1 Begin with a chisel-edge stroke for the first petal.

2 Pull 4 chisel-edge strokes like a clock face at the 3, 6, 9, and 12 o'clock positions. Pull all strokes toward the center.

3 Fill in with the first single layer of petals.

4 In between the first petals, fill in with a second layer of petals that are somewhat shorter and wider than the first layer.

5 Pounce in the centers with a double-loaded scruffy, keeping the darker shading color to one side.

side-facing flowers and buds

1 Paint a fan shape of chisel strokes.

2 Fill in with some shorter chisel strokes.

3 At the base, pull a few green chisel strokes for the calyx.

4 Pull a stem outward from the base, staying up on the chisel edge of the brush.

daisies with wider petals

1 To make petals that are a little wider than the narrow ones found on asters, mums, etc., just press down on the bristles a little more as you paint each chisel stroke.

2 Here's a full daisy with a couple of trailing buds.

3 Pounce in the center of the full daisy with a scruffy, keeping the shading color to one side.

five-petal teardrop flowers

1 Paint three teardrop petals to form a partial flower for the background layer.

2 Overlap the partial with a full five-petal flower.

3 Overlap that one with more five-petal flowers and add a trailing bud or two. Dot in the centers with the tip end of the brush handle.

stalk flowers

1 Stalk flowers is a descriptive term I use for this general shape of flower, including wildflowers such as lavender and veronica, and garden flowers such as statice. Start by painting tall and skinny stems and grass using the chisel edge of the brush. Begin adding the blossoms at the top of the stem with small chisel strokes angled in toward the stem.

2 Continue adding chisel strokes, getting wider and more layered as you go down the stem.

thistles

1 Paint tall thin stems and grass using the chisel edge. For the thistle flowers, stay up on the very tip of the chisel edge, lifting the leading edge slightly; pull spiky strokes outward from the stem in a fan shape. Lead with the lighter color.

2 Flip the brush over so you are leading with the darker side and add another layer of spiky petals.

3 Use a no. 2 script liner with inky paint to make a base for the flower, connecting it to the stem.

tap-tap-tap flowers

1 Paint varying heights of blades of grass using the chisel edge of the brush. Double load your brush with your flower colors. Staying up on the chisel edge, use a tap-tap-tap motion, not a stroking motion, to form the flower clusters. Angle the clusters toward the stem. Brace your little finger on the surface so that your tapping pressure is kept very light.

2 Finish the flower by adding more layers as you go down the stem.

wisteria, lilac or butterfly bush

1 Double load a scruffy brush and pounce the top part of the wisteria blossom in a circular motion, keeping the darker color toward the upper edge and the brush handle straight up and down.

2 Pounce the trailing end of the wisteria blossom by leaning the handle so only the edge touches the surface, but keep the pouncing motion straight up and down to the surface.

1 Begin the pansy by painting a shell stroke for the
back petal with the darker color to the outer edge.

2 Add two more shell-shaped petals for the sides. Keep the lighter side of the
brush to the outside edges of the petals. Turn your work to make painting
these shell strokes easier.

3 The two lower petals are teardrop strokes, keeping the darker
side of the brush to the outside.

4 The center stamens are three little chisel strokes. Finish with a
dot at the base of these three strokes.

pansy bud

1 Start the bud by painting the back petal with a shell stroke.

2 Turn your brush so the lighter color is to the outside and paint a second shell stroke overlapping and slightly below the first stroke. Add two chisel-edge strokes for the side petals with a touch-lean-pull stroke.

4 Pull a stem outward from the base of the bud using the chisel edge of the brush.

3 The base of the bud is a series of little chisel strokes angled toward where the stem will connect.

cabbage rose

1 Double load a ³/₄-inch (19mm) flat with Magenta and Wicker White. Begin the outer skirt with a shell stroke.

2 Complete the outer skirt with more shell strokes that connect to each other at the outer corners of the petals. Turn your work as you paint the circle of petals. Keep the Wicker White side of the brush always to the outside. If you want a full rose with a more centered bud, continue to add shell-stroke layers that get smaller and smaller.

3 Start the center bud slightly below the center petals. Place two guidelines with the chisel edge of your brush. The rest of the rose is built from these guidelines.

4 Form the center bud with an up-and-over stroke for the back of the bud, and a U-stroke for the front. Keep the white side of the brush facing up.

5 Paint a shell stroke on the right side of the bud. Start your brush at the same exact height as the top of the bud at the guideline.

6 Paint a shell stroke on the left side of the bud. Again, start your brush at the same exact height as the top of the bud at the left guideline.

7 Paint more shell strokes to fill in around the front of the bud. The number of shell strokes is based on the size of the rose.

8 Double load a ¾-inch (19mm) angular brush with Wicker White on the toe and Magenta on the heel. Starting on the right guideline at the same height as the top of the bud, lean the white edge of the brush out and slide across the center of the bud.

9 Paint the left side comma-stroke petal using the same procedure as in step 8, but pull from the left, layering this stroke under the first comma stroke.

10 Keeping the Wicker White to the outside, chisel in the final "filler" petal across the front and underneath the two side petals you just painted.

rosebuds and calyx

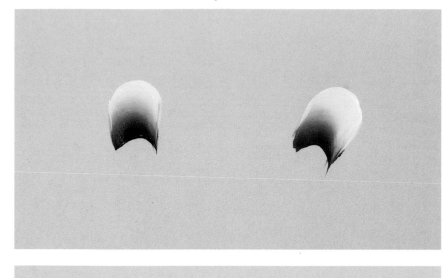

1 Here we are going to paint two types of rose-buds—one tightly closed (on the right) and the other one opening (on the left). Both buds start the same way. Double load a $3/4$-inch (19mm) flat with Magenta and Wicker White. Place two guidelines to start and end the bud, just as you did on the full rose (see step 3 on page 40). Paint the back of each bud with an up-and-over stroke, keeping the Wicker White side of the brush to the top edge.

2 On the tightly closed bud on the right, the front petal is a U-stroke that completes the circle. On the opening bud at the left, the front petal is a U-stroke that comes two-thirds of the way across the back petal. You can go over these strokes a couple of times if you need to.

3 The closed bud has one more U-stroke petal coming all the way across below the previous stroke. The opening bud's front petal is shaped like a boat, and extends beyond the center bud on both sides.

4 The final petal on the closed bud starts in the middle and pulls up and to the right. On the opening bud, begin adding chisel-edge strokes lower on the bud.

5 Continue with the opening bud, chiseling in another petal coming in from the left side. To paint the calyx on the closed bud, load a 3/8-inch (10mm) angular brush with Thicket on the toe and Sunflower on the heel. Starting with the heel of the angular brush at the base of the bud, stroke upward around the side of the bud and continue past it, lifting off to a point. Repeat for the calyx on the other side.

6 To finish the closed bud, paint a center calyx by stroking upward, then pull downward for the stem. To finish the opening bud, chisel stroke two more petals coming in from the right and left sides. Remember to keep the white side of the brush to the outside edges of the petals.

one-stroke leaves, stems and vines

simple one-stroke leaf

1 Double load a ³/₄-inch (19mm) flat with dark green and a lighter green. Touch the chisel edge of the brush to the surface to make two guidelines for the start and end of the one-stroke leaf as shown.

2 Place the chisel edge on the left guideline and press down on the bristles so the flat of the brush is laying on the surface.

3 Turn the dark green side of the brush slightly so it is parallel with the right guideline.

4 Slide forward at the same time as you release the pressure and lift to the chisel, ending the stroke at the right guideline.

wiggle leaf with slide

1 Touch the chisel of the brush to the surface to make two V-shaped guidelines. These will show you where to start each side of the leaf.

2 Press the brush down and wiggle out and in as you turn in a fan-shape direction, pivoting on the lower side to form a shell stroke.

3 When you see the shell shape, stop wiggling and then slide as you lift to the chisel edge to make the leaf tip. On this first half of the leaf, the darker color reaches the tip first, surrounding the lighter color.

4 Start the slide side of the leaf on the other guideline. Lay the bristles down and then slide smoothly as you watch the inside edge of the brush to connect the two halves of the leaf.

5 On this half of the leaf, the lighter color reaches the tip first.

6 Pull a stem halfway in to the center of the leaf, staying up on the chisel and leading with the lighter color.

heart-shaped leaf

1 Begin as you did for the wiggle leaf with slide (see page 45), placing a V-shaped guideline and painting a wiggle-shaped side for the first half of the leaf.

2 Paint the second half using the same procedure. Remember to stop wiggling the brush when you see the shell shape.

3 Slide and lift to the chisel to make the tip. Pull a stem halfway in to the center of the leaf. Notice how the darker color reached the tip first on both halves, thereby surrounding the lighter color.

sunflower leaf

1 Using the chisel edge, place two guidelines that look like an upside-down V. Apply slight pressure and then wiggle out and in. The wiggles for the sunflower leaf are loopier than they are for the heart-shaped leaf. Think about making the letter M.

2 Continue wiggling, angling the brush more as you near the tip. The darker side should reach the tip first.

3 Repeat the above two steps for the other half of the leaf. Pull a stem halfway in to the center.

daisy leaf

1 Using the chisel edge, place two guidelines that look like an upside-down V. These leaves are painted the same way as the sunflower leaves, but the outer edges are more irregular. To do this, just wiggle out a little further in some places than in others.

2 As you get closer to the tip, wiggle less and less, then lift to the chisel and pull to the tip, leading with the darker green side.

3 Repeat for the other half of the leaf, and pull a stem halfway in to the center.

ivy leaf

1 With the chisel, place a V-shaped guideline. Starting on the right side, touch your brush to one guideline, lay the bristles down and paint a wiggle-shaped leaf stroke extending straight out to the side.

2 Touch your brush to the left guideline, lay the bristles down and paint a wiggle-shaped leaf stroke extending straight out to the left side. Place two more V-shaped guidelines over these two leaves as shown.

4 Paint the other half of the leaf the same way. Pull a stem halfway in to the center.

3 Paint one half of a heart-shaped leaf extending downward. Turn and lift to the chisel to pull to the tip.

iris or tulip leaf

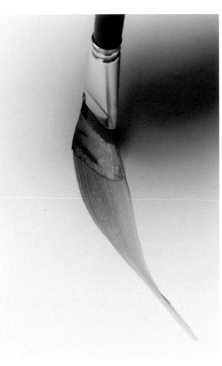

1 Start by pulling the leaf upward from the base, staying up on the chisel edge and leading with the darker green side.

2 Press down on the brush to widen the stroke as you slide the brush at a slightly diagonal angle.

3 Make a kind of hook at the top and then lift up to the chisel edge and turn, reversing your direction and sliding back down.

4 Press down again to widen the stroke.

5 Lift to the chisel and pull to the tip.

fruit leaf

1 With the chisel edge, touch the surface to make a V-shaped guideline. Start on the left guideline and press down as you pivot the brush, turning the darker color around the light color, making a half circle.

2 Lift to the chisel as you slide to the tip. The darker color reaches the tip first.

3 Start the other half of the leaf at the other V guideline. Press down and slide without turning the brush.

4 Slide to the tip as you lift to the chisel. The darker green bristles are the last to lift off the surface.

push-and-pull long leaf

1 This is similar to painting a slide half of a leaf. Push down on the brush, but do not turn or pivot.

2 Pull a long stroke as you lift to the chisel. The longer the leaf, the longer you pull before lifting to the chisel.

shadow leaves

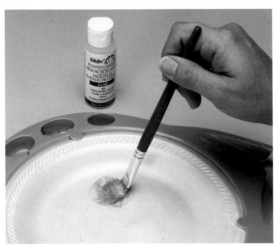

1 Using a dirty brush (one that was loaded previously and then wiped on a paper towel), work in a lot of Floating Medium in a new track until you see a very transparent color. Wipe the brush off on a paper towel or the edge of the palette.

2 Paint a cluster of small one-stroke leaves and stems using the transparent color. Keep these shadow leaves subtle, not too dark. I use shadow leaves in the backgrounds of my paintings to give depth and to fill in any empty areas. Shadow leaves can fill a design without making it look cluttered.

grass blades

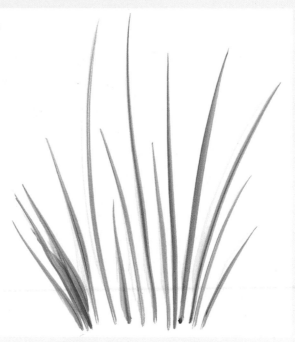

1 Touch the chisel edge to the surface at the bottom where the grass will be. Leading with the lighter color, tilt the handle back slightly and lightly pull upwards, dragging the last few bristles. Your whole arm must move with the stroke—don't just flick the brush with your wrist or your fingers.

2 Here you can see how each blade of grass is highlighted and shaded in one stroke.

vine

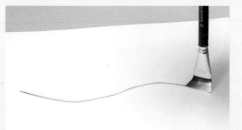

1 Using the chisel edge of a flat brush, lead with the lighter color and paint a curving line.

2 Start at the beginning again to create tendrils. Curve out and away slightly and then cross over the main vine.

3 Start again partway along the main vine, curve outward and cross over the main vine going the opposite way as the previous branching vine. Do not pull the branching vines straight out to the side—it isn't natural-looking.

4 This is how your finished vine should look.

grapevine

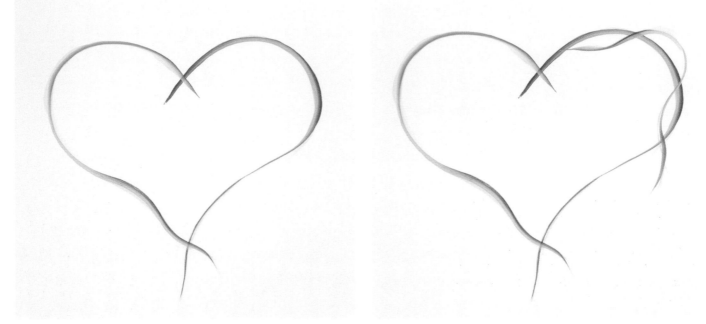

1 Double load a flat brush with a brown color, such as Maple Syrup, and white. Stay up on the chisel edge and pull the brush in whatever shape you like, such as a heart, an arch or a circle, to make a wreath.

2 To create the branching vines, always start on the main vine and pull smaller, curving vines across, weaving back and forth over the main vine as you go.

3 Fill in with as many branching and twisting vines as you like, but always start them on the main vine.

ferns

1 There are two kinds of ferns I like to paint—one with wider leaves that are close together along the stem, and one that has airy, lacy-looking fronds with tiny leaflets. Start by painting a long stem, staying up on the chisel edge and leading with the lighter color. Add smaller branches for the lacy fern that have even smaller branches attached to them.

2 On the wide-leaf fern, add two rows of one stroke leaves. On the lacy fern, the tiny leaves are painted using a short, light daisy stroke, pulling inward toward the stems.

3 When the wide-leaf fern is finished, pull a new stem up the center to clean up the edges. Finish the lacy fern with more leaflets to fill in the frond.

curlicues and string bows

curlicues

2 To change the direction of your circles, without lifting the brush from the surface move the brush in the shape of the letter S, sliding back in the opposite direction, and continue making curls and loops.

1 Curlicues are another way to fill a design without overfilling it. They can also be used to attract the eye to an area that might not have been as noticeable. Curlicues have a way of adding grace and flow to designs as well. Plus they are a needed element when you are painting things such as grapes, pumpkins and ivy. Load a no. 2 script liner with inky color. Brace your little finger on the surface and move your entire arm freely and smoothly. Begin painting a looping, curling line.

3 Don't change direction abruptly—let the line flow fluidly from one direction to the other all along your curlicue.

string bows

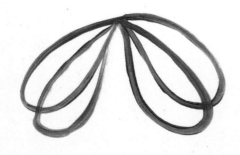

2 Add two hanging ribbons. Tip the liner into white and paint two little C-strokes for the knot.

1 Load a no. 2 script liner with inky paint. Paint two drooping loops on each side.

transferring a pattern

1 Lay a piece of tracing paper over the original drawing or pattern. Trace the larger shapes and important lines, but not the little details like leaf veins or curlicues.

2 Lay the tracing on your surface and secure in two or three places with low-tack tape. Slide a piece of graphite paper, dark side down, underneath the traced pattern. Using a pencil or a stylus, re-trace the lines of the design onto your basecoated surface. Try not to press too hard.

3 Occasionally lift a portion of the pattern and transfer paper to make sure it is transferring correctly.

When the pattern has been completely transferred, you can begin painting. If you are painting elements on top of another shape, such as these flowers on a heart wreath, start by transferring only the shape of the heart. Then paint the heart wreath and allow it to dry before transferring the rest of the design. This way you are not painting the heart wreath on top of the elements that are not painted, thereby obliterating the lines.

beyond one-stroke

painting on paper

There are several new products out on the market that make it easy for artists and crafters to paint on many different kinds of surfaces. Look for these products at your local arts and crafts supply store.

To paint on paper, I use a special paint that is acid-free and archival quality, FolkArt's Papier Paint. Since this paint is thicker than most paints, it requires you to use stiffer-bristled brushes. I use the FolkArt One Stroke Brushes for Paper. You can also use the paint right out of the squeeze bottle, which has a fine applicator tip for drawing, writing or painting delicate lines. Used this way, the paint becomes "dimensional"—in other words, it has body and stands up on the surface.

This kind of paint is perfect for such activities as scrapbooking, making altered art, and creating your own greeting cards. On these two pages, I'll show you how to create a fun and inexpensive card and matching envelope. Just start with plain colored cardstock, and cut the edges of the card with pinking shears or other decorative-edge scissors.

1 Double load a no. 8 paper brush with Papier Paint in Fresh Foliage and Wicker White. Paint a border of one-stroke leaves along the bottom edge of the card. Double load a no. 8 paper brush with Papier Paint in Amethyst Metallic and Wicker White. Paint the flower petals.

2 Use the tip of the paint bottle to add dimensional stamens with Sunflower. Notice how the paint maintains its three-dimensional shape—it does not flatten out unless you stroke it with a brush.

3 Add dimensional stems to the flowers and details to the leaves with Fresh Foliage, using the applicator tip of the bottle. Outline the leaves with the tip of the bottle of Wicker White and add a few more embellishments. Let dry.

4 You can also decorate a matching envelope with this paint. Use the tip of the Papier Paint's Disco Glitter bottle to draw butterfly wings, and then use Fresh Foliage to draw the butterfly's body and antennae.

5 To coordinate the envelope with the card, paint one of the flowers in the lower-right corner. If you like, when the paint is completely dry, cut the bottom of the card along the edge of the leaf design to create a nice customized look.

two-step painting technique

The two-step painting technique is a combination of brush-work and using an applicator bottle to apply dimensional paint. It's a fast and fun way to create all kinds of young-at-heart projects, such as the cigar box purse on page 84, and this china plate painted with updated roses and stripes.

2 Attach a Tip-Pen metal tip and applicator lid to the Enamels paint bottle. Create circles and swirls of white dimensional paint to look like rose petals.

1 Start with a clean, white china plate, and use Enamels paints and brushes specially made for glass and ceramics. Basecoat the circular pink areas for the flowers using a flat brush. Add one-stroke leaves tucked in around the flowers.

3 Outline and detail the leaves with green Enamels using a metal tip on the applicator.

4 Using a large flat Enamels brush, paint wide green stripes around the rim of the plate. Detail the edges of the stripes with wavy lines of white using a metal tip on the applicator.

reverse glass painting technique

Reverse glass painting allows you to paint on the back or underside of a clear glass plate, yet still have the design look right when viewed from the front. It's called "reverse" painting because you paint the design in reverse order from what you usually do on other, nontransparent surfaces. In other words, you will start with the final details first and finish with what normally would be painted first. You must let each step dry before painting the next. Use a blow dryer or heat gun to quicken the drying process. I use FolkArt Enamels paints, which are made for painting on slick surfaces like glass and china.

Even though the Enamels paints are nontoxic, they do not meet the FDA requirements to be considered food safe. This is due to the fact that *any* paint that is applied to glass can be scratched off. The only decorations that are permanent on any glass piece are those that are part of the glassmaking process. They are imbedded into the glass. So if, for instance, you want to use a clear glass platter for serving food but you want to paint it, use the reverse painting technique. If the glass is opaque, then paint on it normally and lay a clear glass plate or plastic wrap on top of the plate to protect the paint.

1 Trace your design onto a piece of paper. Turn your glass plate over on top of your pattern so you can see the pattern through the glass.

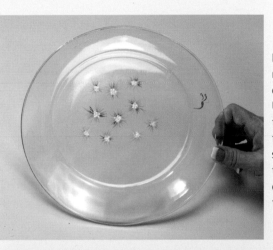

2 Begin by dotting in the yellow centers of the daisies. Paint the green body and antennae of the butterfly on the rim of the plate. Pull tiny Burnt Umber accent lines radiating out from the daisy centers. The picture shows how your plate should look at this point from the back side. Turn your plate over often to check your design from the front.

3 Paint the butterfly wings with yellow and white double-loaded on a flat brush. Paint the white daisy petals, making sure they overlap onto the yellow centers. Remember you are painting on the back of the plate.

4 Turn the plate over and you'll see how the finished design looks from the front. You can see that the daisy centers you painted first are in the right place, and the petals you painted last are behind the centers.

four easy lettering techniques

Adding lettering to your painted projects is a great way to personalize them and give them an elegant finishing touch. In the project on page 85, you'll see how to paint a monogram on the back of a cigar box purse.

Lettering fonts of all styles and sizes can be found on the Internet. Use a photocopier to enlarge or reduce the letters you need. Use tracing paper and graphite paper to transfer your letters to your surface. Or just buy letter stencils at your local craft store.

In the photos below, I'm painting on a piece of tracing paper overlaying my photocopied letter. This is a great way to practice your lettering before painting on an actual surface. Use a flat One Stroke Lettering Brush in the appropriate size for your letters.

fun & funky lettering

1 Load a flat lettering brush with your main color—in this case, a medium blue. Begin by painting all the down strokes and the serifs (cross strokes).

2 Use a lettering liner brush to outline the letter with a darker color to accent the letters and make them pop.

3 This font is fun and funky—great for painting borders or alphabets in kids' rooms.

roman font

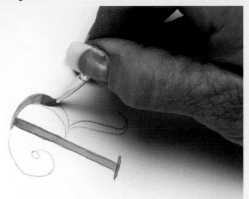

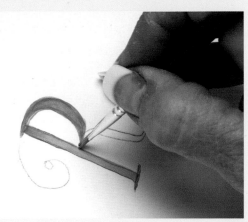

2 Lift back up to the chisel edge to finish the stroke.

1 A "roman" font has letters that are wide in some places and skinny in others, like this "R." Use a flat lettering brush. Start at the top of the curved part of the letter on the chisel edge of the brush, then put pressure on the brush as the curve widens. Do not turn the brush during these strokes. The natural shape of the brush will make the wider and thinner parts without much help from you.

3 Add the curling flourishes with the tip of a lettering liner brush, which has very long bristles to hold a lot of paint.

4 Use the liner and a darker shade of the same color to shade the letter on one side only.

5 The shading gives the letter some depth and dimension.

fancy script lettering

1 For much fancier letters, such as this "B" with lots of curves, use a no. 5 lettering liner, which holds a lot of paint so you don't run out in the middle of a long stroke. Pull the strokes downward, or toward you, turning your surface as needed. Stay on the tip of the brush for the narrower areas and use slight pressure on the brush for the wider areas.

2 Lift back up to the tip and connect to the other stroke. Resist the temptation to overstroke the fine lines of the letter—they'll just get wider.

4 Notice how the strokes cross over and under each other in the lower left where the flourish lines curl and overlap each other. The no. 5 lettering liner allows you to paint these long smooth strokes without stopping to reload.

3 Using a darker shade of the same color, shade along just one side of the letter in the wider areas, not on the skinny flourishes.

Here's how a whole word looks when painted and shaded with lettering brushes. Shading done correctly in the right areas really makes the entire word pop off the background. This kind of lettering is great for projects like signs, mailboxes, floorcloths, or anything else that is seen from a distance.

donna's tips for great design

design #1 leaves and vines

One of the questions that I always get asked is, "How can I make my design flow gracefully?" or "How can I learn to lay out my design better?" In this section, we'll look at four of the most common design problems I see. The first example in each design shows the types of problems many people have when they're first starting out, and the second example shows my solutions. We'll start with the simplest design: leaves and vines.

PROBLEMS

1 Stems too thick from too much pressure on chisel. **2** Leaves too close to vine. **3** Too much pressure on script liner. **4** Leaves sticking straight out to side. **5** Leaves going in wrong direction. **6** Stem pulled all the way to tip of leaf. **7** Leaves are all one color; muddy. **8** Curlicues change direction too abruptly. **9** Curlicues just a series of circles.

problems

solutions

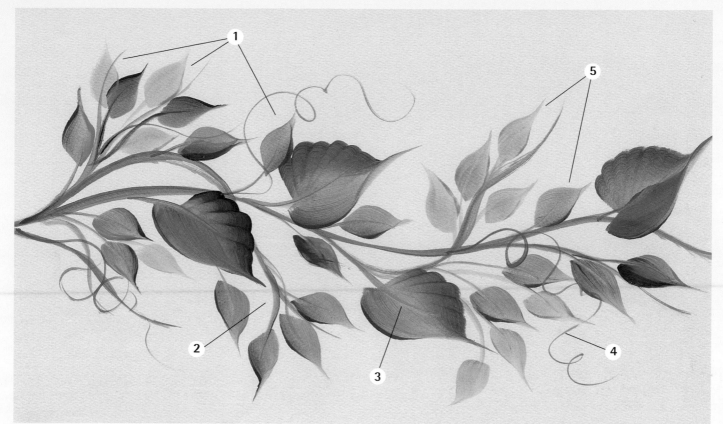

SOLUTIONS

1 Place leaves away from vine, then pull stems. **2** Pull stems on chisel; do not put pressure on brush. **3** Pull stems only halfway into center of leaf. **4** Stay up on tip of script liner when painting curlicues. **5** Leaves should point in the direction of growth.

1 To help you visualize the growth direction of the leaves along the vine, place your open hand along the vine with fingers aimed downward. Your leaves should fall in the same general direction as your fingers.

2 Where the vine curves upward, place your hand with fingers aimed upward. The leaves along this section of the vine should aim in the same general direction as your fingers.

design #2 roses and leaves

More than any other flower, roses are what I am known for. They come in a variety of colors that work well with almost any home decor. The natural beauty of the rose makes it the focal point of any design, regardless of the shape of the design. Since the rose is round, it is limited only by the shape of the surface on which it is painted. And with its range of colors, it can be combined with most other flowers. It's no wonder that I paint a lot of roses!

problems

PROBLEMS

1 Roses are all same size and facing in same direction. **2** Four roses, two buds: even numbers make designs uninteresting. **3** Improperly loaded brush creates harsh dividing lines between colors. **4** Leaf is too dark. **5** Too much yellow. **6** Too much white. **7** Leaves are pointing toward roses rather than away. **8** Leaves too far away from roses. **9** Calyx too thick and curves outward away from bud.

solutions

SOLUTIONS

1 Three roses, three buds—odd numbers create interesting designs. **2** Roses facing in different directions look more natural. **3** Two full-view roses and one half-hidden by leaf creates more intriguing, graceful design. **4** Place buds to fill in design. **5** Paint different-size leaves. **6** Keep largest leaves close to roses. **7** Point all leaves away from center of design. **8** Filler leaves extend your design, soften it, and create depth. **9** Curlicues are subtle and fill in empty areas.

design #3 garden flowers

Other flowers that I love to paint include wildflowers. I like to mix wildflowers and garden flowers in my designs. Florists use wildflowers all the time to fill in their arrangements, so let's use them more often in our designs to add color, shape and interest.

problems

PROBLEMS

1 Too much pressure on brush. **2** Flowers all at exact same height. **3** All petals stroked in at same angle toward center. **4** Same colors grouped together. **5** Daisy petals stroked outward. **6** Daisics all facing front. **7** Too many different types of leaves. **8** Leaves standing straight up like soldiers in a line.

SOLUTIONS

1 Flowers of varying heights are more interesting and natural. **2** Intertwine flower colors to achieve balance. **3** Angle some strokes toward stem, others more downward. **4** Daisies facing different directions—some upward, some sideways, just as in nature. **5** Pull daisy petals in toward center. **6** Paint leaves in same basic shape. **7** Add grass blades to ground the design. **8** Arrange flowers in a more relaxed shape—not stiff and regular.

design #4 fruit border

Over the years I have painted fruit borders in a lot of kitchens, more than I can count. I also designed a fruit border for my own dining room table. Fruit can be painted in bright colors or toned down and antiqued for a quieter, relaxed feeling. I have always combined several different kinds of fruit in my border designs. I know they don't grow that way in nature, but with painting you are your own gardener and there are no rules.

problems

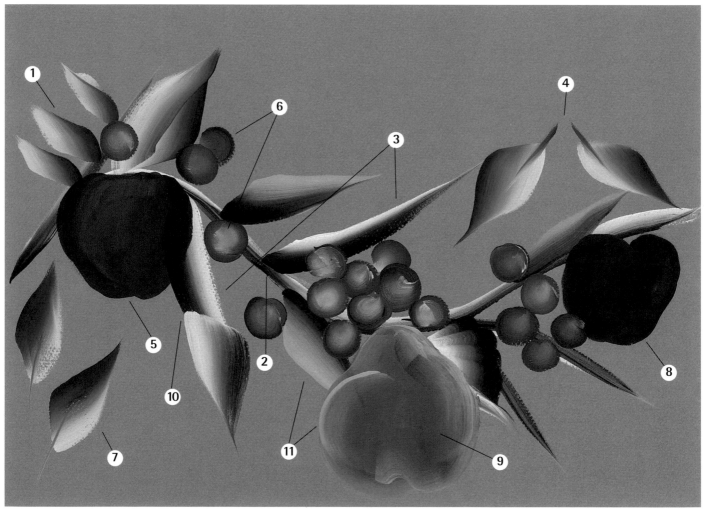

PROBLEMS

1 Leaves sticking straight out from branch. **2** Bad placement of branches. **3** Branches are thicker than vine. **4** Leaves too far away from branch, pointing in wrong direction. **5** Apples and pear are hanging straight down. **6** Grapes are too spread out along vine. **7** Leaves are pointing toward branch. **8** Color is muddy looking—no highlights or shading. **9** Pear is too orange. **10** Leaf extends directly from the end of branch. **11** Colors are not fully blended on brush.

solutions

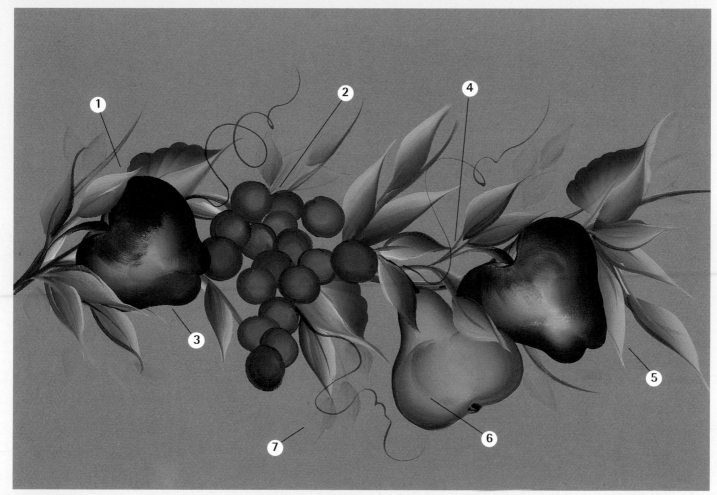

SOLUTIONS
1 Keep bright, vivid colors for fruit leaves. **2** Paint grapes in nice full clusters that hang from vine. **3** Angle fruit in same direction as vines and leaves. **4** Use stems to attach leaves to main vine. **5** All leaves should point outward, in the direction of the growth. **6** Load brush correctly to achieve highlights and shading in one stroke. **7** Add shadow leaves and curlicues to complete design and add depth.

wildflower mailbox

Years ago when I first got married, we couldn't afford to purchase new things for our house. We had to learn to make do with what we had or could purchase at garage sales and flea markets. I began painting to make these things pretty and to give them new life. Painted mailboxes were one of the things that started my business. I began with my own and then surprised my neighbors by painting their mailboxes too. In doing so I realized that mailboxes don't have to be used only for mail. They can be used to decorate your home as well. Here I'm showing you how to paint one of my favorite designs, a cute little birdhouse and wildflowers. This design is sure to make any room cheery or bring a smile to your mail carrier and other visitors.

FolkArt Outdoor Opaque and Outdoor Dimensional Paints

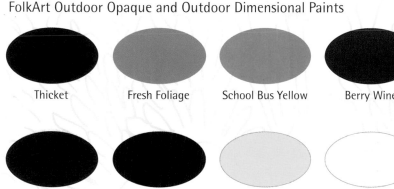

Thicket   Fresh Foliage   School Bus Yellow   Berry Wine

Violet Pansy   Burnt Umber   Lemon Custard (Dimensional)   Wicker White (Opaque and Dimensional)

Surface
- Metal mailbox with brass lid, available at any home improvement center.

Preparation
- Clean with a soft cloth. Trace and transfer the pattern. (Pattern is shown on page 152.)

Brushes: One Stroke for acrylics
- no. 12 flat
- no. 16 flat
- ³/₄-inch (19mm) flat
- ³/₄-inch (19mm) scruffy
- no. 2 script liner

Additional Supplies
- FolkArt Flow Medium for Outdoor Paints
- Spray lacquer in a gloss finish

Foliage and Birdhouse

2 Double load a no. 12 flat with Fresh Foliage and Thicket; paint the one-stroke leaves. Pull stems from the vine into the leaves.

1 Double load a no. 16 flat with Fresh Foliage and Thicket. Using the chisel edge, paint blades of grass and a curving vine; add a few twisting tendrils growing on the main vine.

3 Double load a ³/4-inch (19mm) scruffy with Fresh Foliage and Thicket. Pounce mounds of moss over the bottom edge of the grass.

4 Load a ³/4-inch (19mm) flat into Wicker White and sideload into Burnt Umber. Keeping the Burnt Umber to the outside edge, pull the left side of the birdhouse. Flip the brush over and pull the right side of the birdhouse, overlapping the first stroke rather than painting next to it.

5 Using the same brush and colors, stay up on the chisel and pull a long stroke for the pole. Start at the bottom edge of the birdhouse and pull down.

6 Load a no. 2 script liner with Burnt Umber and pull tiny curving strokes from the sides of the birdhouse inward. Paint a hole with the end of the brush handle, then paint the perch below the hole. Add a highlight to the hole and perch using Wicker White.

7 Load Burnt Umber on a no. 12 flat. Use the chisel edge to pull a base for the birdhouse from the right side toward the center, then pull from the left toward the center, putting a little pressure on the brush to get the width of the base.

8 Double load a no. 12 flat with Berry Wine and Wicker White. Paint the first layer of roof shingles with U-strokes. Angle the two outside strokes to point inward toward the peak of the roof.

9 Continue to add more layers of shingles, painting one less shingle per layer as you go up. Always angle the two outside strokes inward. The topmost shingle is a teardrop stroke.

Stalk Flowers, Daisies and Thistles

10 Begin painting dark and light pink stalk flowers. Double load a no. 12 flat with Berry Wine and Wicker White. Using the chisel edge of the brush and starting at the top of a blade of grass; paint the stalk flowers. For the darker pink flowers, lead with the Wicker White side of the brush. For the lighter pink flowers, lead with the Berry Wine side.

11 The rust-colored flowers are painted with School Bus Yellow and Berry Wine double-loaded on a no. 12 flat. Tap on the chisel edge using very little pressure. Brace with your little finger to prevent pushing too hard on the brush. Start at the top of a blade of grass and layer the flower spikes downward, getting wider as you near the bottom.

12 Load a no. 12 flat with Wicker White; paint the daisy petals by pulling in toward the center of each daisy. Imagine a clock face, and begin with petals at 3, 6, 9, and 12 o'clock. Then fill in with more petals.

13 Outline each daisy petal with the tip end of a bottle of Wicker White Outdoor Dimensional Paint.

14 Dip the end of a brush handle into School Bus Yellow and dot the daisy centers. Add tiny dots around the centers with the tip end of a bottle of Lemon Custard Outdoor Dimensional Paint.

15 To paint the purple thistles, double load a no. 12 flat with Wicker White and Violet Pansy. Stay up on the chisel edge, and leading with the Wicker White side, pull outward from the stem. To give the thistle more depth, turn the brush over and leading with the Violet Pansy side, stroke in more layers of spiky petals. Flip the brush again to make more strokes.

16 Double load a no. 12 flat with Thicket and Fresh Foliage. Leading with the lighter green side, pull stems downward from the thistle blossoms.

17 For the yellow wildflowers, double load a no. 12 flat with Lemon Custard and Wicker White. Stroke layers of petals, angling downward toward the stem. Outline with Wicker White Outdoor Dimensional Paint.

18 The bright yellow flowers at the left are painted just with Lemon Custard Outdoor Dimensional Paint. Make each of the tiny blossoms with pressure-release, pressure-release strokes.

19 Load a no. 2 script liner with Berry Wine and Flow Medium; paint the string bow and ribbon at the base of the birdhouse. Add a little Wicker White for the knot.

20 Load a no. 2 script liner with Thicket and Flow Medium and add curlicues coming off the vine. To paint the wisteria, load a no. 12 flat with Wicker White and Violet Pansy and tap on the blossoms, keeping the white side of the brush toward the outer tip of the blossom. Start tapping at the tip and work your way toward the wider base of the blossom where it connects to the vine.

21 The Outdoor paint is able to withstand normal weather conditions and UV rays. However, if added protection is desired, spray with two or three light coats of a gloss finish lacquer; allow drying time between coats. Make sure the paint has cured for 72 hours prior to spraying.

personal care set

*J*ars and canisters for personal items are great bathroom accessories and painting them makes them beautiful. What a great gift idea for a housewarming or a shower, or just to show how much you care! In this project I'll show you how simple it is to paint a hydrangea design on a set of glass canisters for your bath salts, cotton balls and bubble bath, plus a matching jar candle, using the Enamels paints. They make it easy to paint on slick surfaces and they withstand humid environments like bathrooms and spas. I like to keep the flowers soft looking by using subtle colors.

FolkArt Enamels Paints

Thicket   Italian Sage   Lemon Custard

Periwinkle   Wicker White

Surfaces
- Large, medium and small lidded glass canisters. Lidded glass jar candle, available at home centers or candle stores.

Preparation
- Clean with a soft cloth. Tape pattern to inside of canister. Or trace pattern onto outside of jar candle. (Pattern is shown on page 152.)

Brushes: One Stroke Enamel
- no. 12 flat
- no. 16 flat
- ³/₄-inch (19mm) flat
- no. 2 script liner

Additional Supplies
- FolkArt Enamels Clear Medium

Leaves and Hydrangea Petals

1 Double load a ³/₄-inch (19mm) flat with Italian Sage and Thicket and paint the large background leaves. Load a no. 12 flat with Italian Sage and paint the smaller one-stroke leaves. Wipe the brush off on a paper towel and then work in a lot of Clear Medium. Blend well until you see a transparent color; paint some shadow one stroke leaves.

2 Double load a no. 12 flat with Periwinkle and Wicker White and begin painting the hydrangea florets, using a teardrop stroke to create each petal.

3 Continue making teardrop strokes, ending each stroke at the center point. Your completed floret should have five or six individual petals.

5 Paint the trailing buds starting with a touch-and-lean. Touch the brush to the surface...

4 Layer the florets to create depth and make the hydrangea blossom look more rounded. Start on the outer edges of the cluster with partial florets and work toward the center, making the florets in the center complete.

6 ...then pull that stroke, lifting up at the end to form a point.

Hydrangea Centers and Butterfly

7 Dip the handle end of the brush into Lemon Custard and dot the centers of the florets.

8 To create a nice finishing touch, paint a few hydrangea florets on the lid of the canister, using the same brushes and colors. Let the paint dry and cure completely before filling with your favorite personal care items.

9 The jar candle has a slightly different design that wraps around the jar. I added a butterfly on the jar and on the lid. Double load a no. 16 flat with Thicket and Wicker White. Paint the vine that encircles the jar, then paint the leaves.

10 Load a no. 12 flat with Periwinkle and Wicker White; paint the florets. For variety and interest, keep the white to the outside edge on some of the florets, and on others flip the brush over so the Periwinkle is to the outside for darker florets. Dot the centers with Lemon Custard.

11 To paint the butterflies, double load a no. 12 flat with Lemon Custard and Wicker White. Paint the back wing first, then the front wing, then the two lower wings. Use a no. 2 script liner with Thicket that has been thinned slightly with Clear Medium to paint the body, head and antennae.

wild rose cigar box purse

*C*igar box purses are a great accessory you can customize to match your outfit. What better way to show off your painting skills than with a purse you painted? This purse has a wild rose design on one side, and a monogram on the other. You can find many different lettering styles on the Internet or look in the craft stores for lettering stencils. Cigar box purses come in a variety of styles with lots of handles to choose from. Or make your own handles out of beads or cord. The possibilities are endless. Check in your local craft store, thrift store or tobacco store for authentic cigar boxes. You can protect your painted purse from wear by applying a couple of coats of spray lacquer, allowing it to dry between coats.

FolkArt Acrylics and Outdoor Dimensional Paints

Thicket

Fuchsia

Fresh Foliage

Light Fuchsia

School Bus Yellow

Wicker White
(Acrylic and Outdoor
Dimensional)

Surface
- Wooden cigar box purse with faux bamboo handle from crafts supply store.

Preparation
- Clean with a soft cloth. Trace and transfer the wild rose pattern onto one side of the purse. (Pattern is shown on page 152.)

Brushes: One Stroke for acrylics
- no. 8 flat
- no. 16 flat
- 1/2-inch (12mm) scruffy
- no. 2 script liner

One Stroke Lettering Brushes
- no. 2 flat
- no. 5 script liner

Additional Supplies
- FolkArt Floating Medium
- Spray lacquer in matte, satin or gloss finish

Leaves and Wild Rose

1 Double load a no. 16 flat with Fresh Foliage and Thicket; paint the large wiggle leaves and the larger one-stroke leaves.

2 Double load a no. 16 flat with Fuchsia and Wicker White and paint the two skirts for the wild rose; then paint the petals for the side-facing rose and the rosebud.

3 Double load a ¹/₂-inch (12mm) scruffy with School Bus Yellow and Wicker White, then add a touch of Thicket to the Wicker White edge. Pounce the center of the wild rose, keeping the Thicket to the outside edge.

5 Dip the tip of the script liner into School Bus Yellow and Wicker White and dot lots of little anthers on the ends of the stamens.

4 Load a no. 2 script liner with inky Thicket and pull lots of little stamens out from the Thicket edge of the center.

6 Double load a no. 8 flat with Fresh Foliage and Thicket, then pick up a little bit of Wicker White. Paint little one-stroke leaves and stems, and calyxes on the buds. Load a no. 2 script liner with inky Thicket and outline the leaves and the stems.

Border, Outlining and Monogram

7 Paint a border around the edge of the purse with a no. 2 script liner loaded with inky Fresh Foliage. Paint a straight border line first. To keep this line a consistent distance from the edge, brace your little finger against the side of the cigar box as you pull the line.

8 Go over the straight line border with a freehand wavy line. Make this wavy line look like a vine weaving in and out.

9 Using the tip end of the Wicker White Outdoor Dimensional Paint, outline the edges of all the wild rose petals, making them very ruffly.

10 Load a no. 16 flat with Light Fuchsia and work Floating Medium into the brush. Pull wide pink stripes across all four sides of the cigar box. Load Fresh Foliage onto a no. 16 and, using the chisel edge, paint thin stripes between the wide pink ones. If you wish, you can personalize the other side of the cigar box purse with a monogram. After tracing your monogram onto the purse, load a no. 2 flat lettering brush with Fresh Foliage and paint all the downward strokes first.

11 Load a no. 5 script liner lettering brush with inky Fresh Foliage and paint the curving and connecting strokes.

12 Shade one side of each letter with inky Thicket on a no. 5 or a no. 2 script liner. Keep the shading on the same side of each letter. This will give your letters some depth and help them pop.

daisy flowerpots

*T*erra cotta pots are not just for the garden anymore! We use the big pots to hold cold sodas when we have our family get-togethers. They can easily be used for centerpieces or other decorative accessories. When I had a booth at a craft fair, the most popular thing I sold were my painted flowerpots. They would sell so fast that the booth turned into a family affair. My children were put to work basecoating, and my husband would sell the pieces as fast as I could paint them! In this project I'll show you three styles of daisies that you can easily paint any color you like. I basecoated these pots first with dark green. Using light colors on a dark green background really makes the colors pop! Notice how I turned the lighter green to the outside edges of the leaves? This is a great technique to use on dark surfaces.

FolkArt Outdoor Opaque Paints

Thicket	School Bus Yellow	Wicker White	Fuchsia

Lemon Custard	Burnt Umber	Yellow Ochre

Surfaces
- 3 terra cotta flowerpots from any garden center.

Preparation
- Clean with a soft cloth. Trace and transfer the patterns. (Patterns are shown on page 153.)

Brushes: One Stroke for acrylics
- no. 12 flat
- no. 16 flat
- 3/4-inch (19mm) flat
- 1/4-inch (6mm) scruffy

Additional Supplies
- FolkArt Flow Medium for Outdoor Paints
- Spray lacquer in a satin finish

Pink Daisies with Narrow Petals

  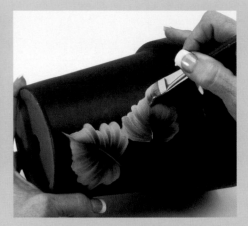

1 Double load a ³/₄-inch (19mm) flat with Thicket and School Bus Yellow, and pick up a little Wicker White on the School Bus Yellow side. Paint the large leaves, keeping the yellow side of the brush to the outside edge of the leaf.

2 Flatten your brush and wiggle up, slide down, wiggle up, slide down, to create the ruffled, uneven edges of the leaves.

3 Paint the other half of the leaf, watching the yellow side of your brush as you draw the shape. Lift up to the chisel edge as you slide to the tip.

  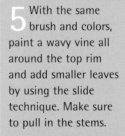

5 With the same brush and colors, paint a wavy vine all around the top rim and add smaller leaves by using the slide technique. Make sure to pull in the stems.

4 Pull a stem into the center of each leaf, staying up on the chisel edge of the brush.

6 Load a no. 16 flat with Fuchsia and Wicker White; pull skinny daisy petals in toward the center, leading with the Fuchsia. Use very little pressure to keep these petals skinny.

7 Fill in the first round of petals, and then paint a second layer of petals all around.

8 Continue to add a few more fully open daisies and some side-facing daisies. Fill in the rim with small, opening buds.

9 Load a 1/4-inch (6mm) scruffy with Lemon Custard and then add a touch of Yellow Ochre to one side. Pounce the daisy centers, keeping the Yellow Ochre to the outside to shade.

10 Double load a no. 12 flat with Lemon Custard and Thicket. Paint the bases and stems for the side-facing daisies.

11 Here is how your finished pink-daisies flowerpot should look. Repeat this design on the other side so your flowerpot looks great all around.

Yellow Daisies with Wide Petals

12 Double load a ³⁄₄-inch (19mm) flat with Thicket and School Bus Yellow; add a touch of Wicker White to the School Bus Yellow side. Paint the large leaves, keeping the yellow side of the brush to the outside edge of the leaf. Add a few comma strokes above the leaves.

13 Make sure the comma strokes are spaced so there is enough room for the daisy blossoms to fit in.

14 Double load a no. 12 flat with School Bus Yellow and Wicker White; add a touch of Yellow Ochre to the School Bus Yellow side. Pull daisy petals in toward the center, using more pressure to make wider petals than you did for the pink daisies.

15 The side-facing daisies are just three or four strokes pulled toward a point at the base.

16 Load a ¹⁄₄-inch (6mm) scruffy with Yellow Ochre and then add a touch of Burnt Umber to one side. Pounce the daisy centers, keeping the Burnt Umber to the outside to add shading.

White Daisies

17 Double load a ³/₄-inch (19mm) flat with Thicket and School Bus Yellow; add a touch of Wicker White on the School Bus Yellow side. Paint the large leaves, keeping the yellow side of the brush to the outside edges of the leaves. Use a no. 12 flat with the same colors to paint the smaller leaves and a few comma strokes.

18 Load a no. 12 flat with only Wicker White. Touch, lean and pull to the center to make the white daisy petals. Paint a few fully open daisies, and then paint some side-facing buds.

19 Load a ¼-inch (6mm) scruffy with School Bus Yellow; add a touch of Thicket to one side. Pounce the daisy centers, keeping the green to the outside for shading.

20 When all your paint is dry, protect your flowerpots with several coats of a spray lacquer in a satin finish, allowing each coat ample time to dry before applying the next.

fruit and plaid tile tray

$\mathcal{W}$hat better way to serve refreshing summer beverages than on a tray painted with fruit that looks good enough to eat! The Enamels paints I used for this project are made for nonporous surfaces, and ceramic tiles are just that. I painted this fruit using bright colors, but you can tone them down with a touch of brown in the leaves, burgundy in the apple or burnt sienna in the pear. Experiment with different colors to suit your taste and décor.

FolkArt Enamels Paints

Engine Red	Lemon Custard	Thicket	Fresh Foliage
Midnight	Burnt Umber	Yellow Ochre	Berry Wine
Violet Pansy	Wicker White		

Surface
- Twelve 4-inch (10cm) square, bisque-colored glazed tiles with matte finish.

Preparation
- Clean tiles with a soft cloth. Trace and transfer the patterns. (Patterns are shown on page 153.)

Brushes: One Stroke Enamel
- nos. 6, 8, 12 and 16 flats
- no. 2 script liner

Additional Supplies
- FolkArt Flow Medium
- FolkArt Enamels Clear Medium
- Liquid Nails clear adhesive
- White bathroom caulk
- White wooden picture frame
- Luan or other thin plywood
- Metal handles with screws

Apple Tile

1 Double load two-thirds of a no. 16 flat with Engine Red and one-third with Lemon Custard. Using the flat side of the brush with Engine Red to the outer edge, begin painting the apple. Start with the indentation at the top of the apple.

2 Continue stroking around the right side of the apple and shape the bottom dimple before lifting the brush.

3 Pick up fresh paint and, starting again at the top on the left side of the indentation...

4 ...paint the left side of the apple. Make sure to cross over the bottom dimple again. This keeps the two halves blended.

5 Using the same brush and colors and keeping the Engine Red to the right side, pull strokes down from the top right edge to fill in the right center area. Then flip the brush over and fill in the left center area. This keeps the highlight in the center of the apple.

hint

When painting with the Enamels brushes, you do not need to press as hard as you would if you were using the acrylics brushes.

6 Don't overblend these center strokes—keep them streaky to look like the skin of a real apple.

7 Side load fresh Engine Red and re-emphasize the dimple at the top of the apple with a short curved stroke that looks like a smile.

9 Double load a no. 16 flat with Thicket and Fresh Foliage; add a touch of Lemon Custard to the Fresh Foliage side. Pull a stem outward from the top indentation on the apple using a touch-lean-pull motion.

8 Wipe the brush on a paper towel and then pick up Engine Red on the tips of the chisel edge. Change your grip on the brush to hold it lightly further back on the handle; touch and pull some light streaky lines from the dimple line down. Try not to make these opaque; you still want to see yellow in the middle.

10 Using the same brush and colors, add the three leaves on the top of the apple.

Blueberry Tile

1 Double load a no. 16 flat with Thicket and Fresh Foliage; add a touch of Lemon Custard to the Fresh Foliage side. Paint the large leaves. Load a no. 8 flat with Fresh Foliage and paint the smaller leaves. Load a no. 2 script liner with an inky mixture of Thicket and Flow Medium; paint curlicues.

2 Load a no. 8 flat with Wicker White, then side load with Midnight. Keeping the Midnight to the outside edge, paint a half circle to start a blueberry.

4 Layer the berries in a cluster, making sure to have some darker than others.

5 Load a no. 6 flat with Midnight and paint a little seed pod on the end of each blueberry.

3 Flip the brush and paint the second half of the blueberry. Do this for each berry.

6 Pick up fresh Wicker White on your brush and dab a highlight on each seed pod.

hint
When using Enamels paints, work quickly so the paint doesn't dry.

Pear Tile

1 Load a no. 16 flat with Lemon Custard, then sideload with Yellow Ochre. Paint the top portion of the pear.

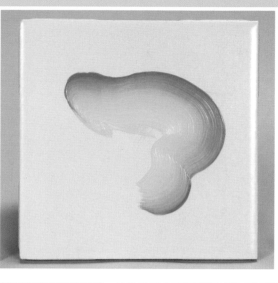

2 Continue along the right side of the pear and on down to the indentation at the bottom, keeping the Yellow Ochre side of the brush to the outside edge of the pear at all times.

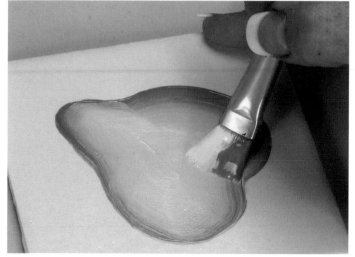

3 Pick up fresh paint and, starting at the right side of the top, re-stroke the top and then continue around the left side of the pear. Keep your eye on the Yellow Ochre side of the brush as you draw the shape of the pear. Make sure to cross over the bottom indentation to the other side.

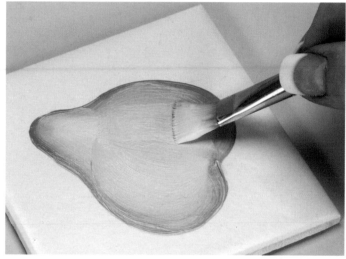

4 Fill in the center of the pear, keeping the lightest yellow in the center for the highlight.

5 Sideload the same brush with fresh Yellow Ochre and shade the bulbous shape of the pear.

6 Double load a no. 16 flat with Thicket and Fresh Foliage; add a touch of Lemon Custard to the Fresh Foliage side. Paint the leaves and stems, then add a few dots at the blossom end with the corner of the brush.

Plum Tile

1 Double load a no. 16 flat with Violet Pansy and Wicker White; paint a large C-shape with the Violet Pansy to the outside edge. Do not turn the brush, just move it in a C-shape.

2 Pick up fresh paint and paint a teardrop stroke on top of the C-shape to complete the plum.

3 Paint another plum overlapping the first one, at a slightly different angle.

4 The leaves and stems are painted with Thicket, Fresh Foliage and Lemon Custard, just as you did on the pear. Stay up on the chisel edge to paint the stems.

Cherries Tile

2 Begin painting a second cherry.

1 Load a no. 12 flat with Engine Red; paint a C-shaped stroke. Pick up fresh paint and paint a second C-shape, overlapping the first, then flip the brush to paint a backward C to finish the cherry.

3 Flip the brush over and paint the other half of the circle to complete the second cherry.

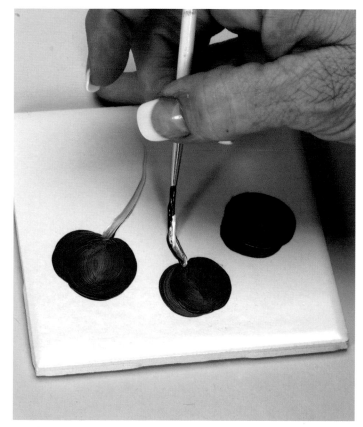

4 Paint a third cherry. Load a no. 2 script liner with Burnt Umber and Wicker White; pull three stems away from the cherries.

5 Double load a no. 16 flat with Thicket and Fresh Foliage. Add a touch of Lemon Custard to the Fresh Foliage side, and paint the leaves and stems.

Blackberries Tile

1 Double load a no. 16 flat with Thicket and Fresh Foliage and add a touch of Lemon Custard to the Fresh Foliage side; paint the larger leaves and stems. Paint the smaller leaves with a no. 8 flat and the curlicues with a no. 2 script liner and inky Thicket.

2 Double load a no. 16 flat with Berry Wine and Violet Pansy. Add a touch of Wicker White to the chisel edge and blend to soften both colors. Paint teardrop shapes, keeping the Violet Pansy side to the outside edge.

4 Overlap the segments to fill in the berries and give them a rounded shape. Let the segments overlap the edge of the basecoat as well.

3 To paint the individual berry segments, load a no. 6 flat with Violet Pansy and sideload with Wicker White. Paint little U-shaped strokes starting at the bottom. Occasionally pick up a little Berry Wine for variation.

5 Double load a no. 6 flat with Thicket and Fresh Foliage; paint tiny one stroke leaves to form a calyx. Load a no. 2 script liner with Fresh Foliage; pull stems out from the calyxes to finish.

Plaid Tiles

1 Wipe the surface of your tiles with rubbing alcohol to clean. Load a no. 16 flat with Wicker White and then work in some Clear Medium. Paint wide white stripes on six of the tiles. These will have the plaid design.

2 Use the chisel edge of the no. 16 flat to paint the white pinstripes on the tiles.

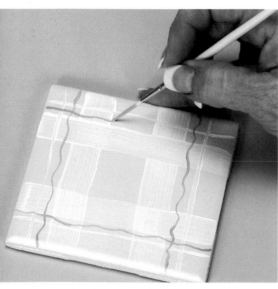

3 Load a no. 2 script liner with an inky mixture of Flow Medium and Fresh Foliage. Wiggle thin green lines across each tile to finish the plaid design.

Buy a wooden picture frame that fits the assembled tiles or cut molding to fit. Attach a thin piece of luan or other plywood backing to the frame to form a tray. Glue the painted tiles to the backing board with Liquid Nails clear adhesive. Caulk between the tiles with white bathroom caulk. Attach a handle on each side of the tray using screws.

wildflower wall cabinet

Wreaths are another versatile design idea and are so easy to paint using the One-Stroke technique. They can be painted round, oval or heart-shaped. Floral designers use wreaths for all types of decoration and for any occasion. Here I painted a heart-shaped wreath on cabinet doors. Imagine this cabinet in a powder room or a bathroom, or change the colors a little and display it in a country kitchen.

FolkArt Acrylics and Artists' Pigments

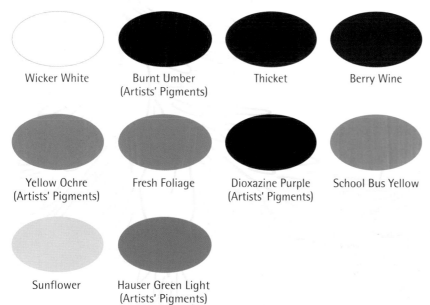

Wicker White

Burnt Umber
(Artists' Pigments)

Thicket

Berry Wine

Yellow Ochre
(Artists' Pigments)

Fresh Foliage

Dioxazine Purple
(Artists' Pigments)

School Bus Yellow

Sunflower

Hauser Green Light
(Artists' Pigments)

Surface

- White wall cabinet, available at stores that sell home furnishings and accessories.

Preparation

- Clean with a soft cloth. Trace and transfer the pattern onto the doors. (Pattern is shown on page 154.)

Brushes: One Stroke for acrylics

- no. 12 flat
- no. 16 flat
- ³/₄-inch (19mm) flat
- ³/₄-inch (19mm) scruffy
- ¹/₄-inch (6mm) scruffy
- no. 2 script liner

Additional Supplies

- FolkArt Floating Medium
- Spray lacquer in a satin or gloss finish

Heart-shaped Wreath

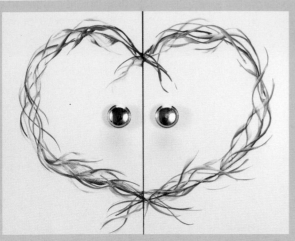

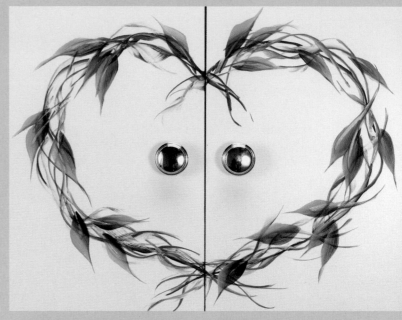

1 Double load a ³/₄-inch (19mm) flat brush with Burnt Umber and Wicker White, and then work some Floating Medium into the brush. Paint the grapevine wreath on the cabinet doors. Refer to page 54 for detailed instructions.

2 Double load the same brush with Thicket and Burnt Umber, picking up a little bit of Wicker White. Paint the long, slender one-stroke leaves around the grapevine, keeping all of the leaves pointing out away from the top center.

3 Load a no. 2 script liner with inky Dioxazine Purple and paint the bow and ribbon.

4 Load a no. 12 flat with Berry Wine and Wicker White and paint the back petals of the rosebuds.

5 Using the same brush and colors, paint the front petals.

Yellow and Purple Flowers

6 Load a no. 12 flat with Burnt Umber and Wicker White; use the chisel edge to paint the stems of the yellow yarrow flowers.

7 Double load a ¾-inch (19mm) scruffy brush with Yellow Ochre and Wicker White; pounce to form the yarrow blossoms.

8 Double load a no. 12 flat with Berry Wine and Wicker White, then sideload with Dioxazine Purple. Paint the petals of the purple five-petal flowers using teardrop strokes.

9 Dot in the centers of the purple flowers with a no. 2 script liner loaded with Thicket and School Bus Yellow.

Pink Trumpet Flowers and Yellow Daisies

10 Double load a no. 16 flat with Berry Wine and Wicker White; paint the pink trumpet flowers. Paint the bud first, then the base of the full trumpets, and then the back petal of the trumpets.

11 Load a no. 2 script liner with inky Fresh Foliage and Thicket and pull the stamens. Pick up a little School Bus Yellow on the brush and paint the anthers on the tips of the stamens.

12 Double load a no. 16 flat with Berry Wine and Wicker White. Paint the front petal of the trumpets by wiggling the brush to make the ruffle at the edge of the petal, then pull strokes back toward the base using the chisel edge of the brush to blend.

14 Load a ¼-inch (6mm) scruffy brush with Yellow Ochre and then pick up a touch of School Bus Yellow on one side and Berry Wine on the other side. Pounce the centers of the daisies at the top of the cabinet. Double load a no. 12 flat with Yellow Ochre and Wicker White; paint the yellow five-petal flowers. Keep the Yellow Ochre to the outer edges of the petals.

13 Double load a no. 12 flat with Yellow Ochre and Wicker White; add a touch of Sunflower on the Yellow Ochre side and paint the daisy petals. The daisy petals at the bottom of the cabinet door are a double-load of Yellow Ochre and Berry Wine.

Purple Statice and Butterflies

15 Load a no. 2 script liner with inky Burnt Umber and dot around the centers. While these are wet, pull spiky lines into the petals to define them. Highlight the centers with Sunflower.

16 To paint the purple statice, first paint a green stem using Thicket. Then pull in short strokes of Dioxazine Purple and Wicker White for the petals. Refer to page 36 for more information on painting stalk flowers.

17 Double load a no. 12 flat with Fresh Foliage and Thicket and add a few new leaves, occasionally pick up a little Wicker White on your brush. Use the same colors to add calyxes where needed. Finish off with a couple of butterflies painted with Dioxazine Purple and Wicker White, and additional curlicues painted with inky Thicket.

18 Load a 3/4-inch (19mm) flat with Hauser Green Light and paint short stripes along the horizontal edges of the cabinet above and below the doors and above the towel rod. When all your paint is dry, protect your cabinet with several coats of a glossy or satin spray lacquer, depending on the finish of your cabinet.

cabbage rose table setting

*T*he secret to successful glass painting is to always load your brush with a lot of paint and lay the paint onto the glass rather than stroking and re-stroking. The Enamels paints are made for nonporous surfaces and can be baked or air cured for 21 days. They can be washed in the top shelf of the dishwasher, but I still recommend gentle hand-washing for longer lasting results. The paint is nontoxic, but it does not meet the FDA requirements to be considered food safe. If you want to use your painted plate for serving food, cover it with plastic wrap or place a clear glass plate on top. If you're painting glasses or mugs, keep the design at least one inch below the rim.

FolkArt Enamels Paints

Thicket

Lemon Custard

Wicker White

Magenta

Fresh Foliage

Hauser Green Medium

Plum Vineyard

Surfaces
- 12-inch (31cm) clear glass plate
- 12-inch (31cm) white china charger

Preparation
- Clean with a soft cloth dampened with rubbing alcohol. Trace and transfer the rose pattern. (Pattern is shown on page 155.)

Brushes: One Stroke Enamel
- no. 12 flat
- no. 16 flat
- ³/₄-inch (19mm) flat
- ³/₄-inch (19mm) scruffy
- no. 2 script liner

Additional Supplies
- FolkArt Enamels Clear Medium

Cabbage Rose

1 Clean the clear glass plate with rubbing alcohol. Be careful not to get your fingerprints on the side of the glass to be painted. Double load a ³/₄-inch (19mm) flat with Magenta and Wicker White; paint the outer skirt of the main rose in the center of the plate. Also paint the two back petals of the rosebuds, and then the outer skirt of the side facing rose. See pages 40-41 for detailed instructions on painting a cabbage rose.

2 Using the same brush and colors, continue painting the cabbage rose and the side-facing rose with the next layer of petals, and then paint the centers of the rosebuds. Work quickly so the paint doesn't dry.

3 Continue adding layers of petals to the rose-bud and the side-facing rose. Remember to always load your brush with a lot of paint and lay the paint onto the glass rather than stroking and re-stroking.

4 Paint the comma strokes around the center bud of the cabbage rose and the side-facing rose. Add the final outside layer of petals to the rosebuds.

5 Double load a ³/₄-inch (19mm) flat with Thicket and Fresh Foliage, add a touch of Wicker White to the Fresh Foliage side. Paint the large leaves. Load the no. 12 flat to paint the smaller leaves, the calyxes on the rosebuds, and the stems. Load the no. 2 script liner with inky Thicket and paint the curlicues.

6 Double load a large scruffy with Plum Vineyard and Wicker White; pounce to form the wisteria. Don't over-pounce; you want to see all the various shades of purple and white.

Green Plaid Charger and Yellow Butterflies

7 Be sure the surface of your white china charger is clean and free of dust. Load a ³/₄-inch (19mm) flat with Clear Medium and then add Fresh Foliage; paint the widest green stripes on the charger first.

8 Use the chisel edge of a ³/₄-inch (19mm) flat loaded with Thicket; paint the dark green stripes.

9 Double load a no. 12 flat with Lemon Custard and Wicker White and paint the wings of the yellow butterflies. Paint the body and antennae with the no. 2 script liner loaded with Thicket. Place the green plaid charger behind your rose-painted plate for a fresh and spring-like table setting!

Roses on Glassware

1 To create a matching place setting, paint drinking glasses with a variation of the same design. Load a no. 16 flat with Hauser Green Medium and dip into Clear Medium and blend. Paint wide vertical stripes starting at the base to about halfway up the glass. Load the same brush with Hauser Green Medium and a touch of Wicker White; paint a vine and leaves.

2 Load a no. 12 flat with Magenta and Wicker White; paint the open rose buds.

3 Load a no. 12 flat with Wicker White and paint the filler flowers. Stay up on the chisel edge and tap the blossoms lightly, angling them toward the vine.

4 The same rose design can be painted on any shape of glassware such as this goblet. You can also paint a plaid motif on the underside of the base to coordinate with the green plaid charger.

sunflower garden tools

*G*ardening tools can be very drab and boring to look at, so it's no wonder that we keep them in a shed out of sight. With the development of the new Outdoor paints, you can turn your garden tools into useful and beautiful pieces that you can leave out all year long. Outdoor paints are perfect for painting on this galvanized metal watering can, garden pail, mini-trowel and cultivator. With these projects, I'll show you easy ways to make your garden tools look as pretty as the flowers they tend.

FolkArt Outdoor Opaque and Outdoor Dimensional Paints

Thicket
(Opaque)

School Bus Yellow
(Opaque)

Yellow Ochre
(Opaque)

Maple Syrup
(Opaque)

Licorice
(Opaque)

Wicker White
(Opaque and
Dimensional)

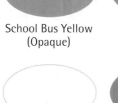
Fresh Foliage
(Dimensional)

Lemon Custard
(Dimensional)

Surfaces

- Galvanized metal watering can
- Galvanized metal garden pail
- Mini-cultivator and trowel

Preparation

- Wipe the galvanized metal surfaces with rubbing alcohol and let dry. Trace and transfer the patterns. (Patterns are shown on page 155.)

Brushes: One Stroke for acrylics

- no. 12 flat
- 3/4-inch (19mm) flat
- 3/4-inch (19mm) scruffy
- no. 2 script liner

Additional Supplies

- Spray lacquer in a matte, satin or gloss finish

Sunflower Watering Can

3 Double load a no. 12 flat with Yellow Ochre and School Bus Yellow. Grab the wet edge of the sunflower center and push, turn and pull each petal outward away from the center, lifting to the chisel to form the tip of the petal.

1 Double load a ¾-inch (19mm) scruffy with Maple Syrup and Licorice. Keeping the Maple Syrup side up, pounce the center of the sunflower by moving in a C-shape, starting at the right side and pouncing up and over and around to form the top part of the center.

2 Finish the center by continuing around the lower part of the center. Connect to the starting point.

4 Continue painting petals all around, grabbing the wet edge of the center every time. Make sure to pick up fresh yellow paint to keep the petal colors bright.

5 After all the petals are painted, reload the ¾-inch (19mm) scruffy with Maple Syrup and Licorice and re-pounce the center to cover the inner edges of the petals, making the center look like it is on top.

Leaves and Daisies

6 Using the same colors, add a smaller, side-view sunflower to the right of the large one. After re-pouncing the center, do not wash the scruffy yet. Paint a bud to the left of the main flower with a few petal strokes. There is no center pounced for the bud.

7 Add a touch of Yellow Ochre to the Maple Syrup side of the still-loaded scruffy and pounce a C-shaped highlight on the center of the large sunflower. On the side-view sunflower, pounce on a round-shaped highlight to the top left part of the center.

8 Double load a ³/₄-inch (19mm) flat with School Bus Yellow and Thicket; paint the large leaves and stems. Use a no. 12 flat and the same colors to paint the smaller one-stroke leaves.

9 Load a no. 12 flat with Wicker White. Add some white daisies here and there around the sunflowers and overlapping some of the leaves. Pull all the daisy petal strokes in toward the center. For variety and interest, make some of the daisies side-facing, some fully open, and some buds.

10 Use the end of the handle to dot the centers with School Bus Yellow.

Garden Pail and Bumblebee

11 Using the same brushes and colors, paint the sunflower on the galvanized metal garden pail using the same procedures as on the watering can (see page 118), but leave off a few petals along the top to make the sunflower look like it's turned upward slightly.

12 Double load a ³/₄-inch (19mm) flat with Thicket and School Bus Yellow and paint the leaves using the same procedures as on the watering can.

13 Double load a no. 12 flat with School Bus Yellow and Yellow Ochre. Touch, lean and pull to paint the body of the bumblebee. This is the same stroke as a one-stroke leaf.

14 Dip the handle end into Licorice and place a dot for the bumblebee's head.

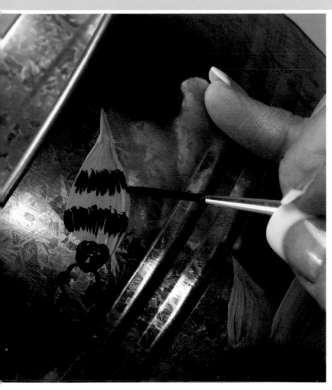

15 Load the no. 2 script liner with Licorice; paint the antennae and then paint little stripes on the body.

16 Load a no. 12 flat with Wicker White, then sideload with a touch of Licorice; blend well to create a soft gray. Paint two wings on both sides of the body. Note: the wings are painted like little one-stroke leaves.

18 Load a no. 12 flat with Wicker White; paint daisies around the rim of the pail. Dot the centers with School Bus Yellow.

17 If you wish, add a couple of bumblebees to the top of the watering can, using the same brushes and colors you used on the garden pail. You can also add motion lines to show the movement of the bumblebees. The motion lines are painted with a no. 2 script liner and inky Licorice. Move your script liner in a random curving line and let it break here and there.

Outlining with Dimensional Paint

19 Add a fresh and fun look to your garden tools by using the Outdoor Dimensional paints. The applicator tip on these squeeze bottles allows you to draw fine lines—no brush is needed. Outline the leaves on the garden pail using Fresh Foliage Outdoor Dimensional paint. Be loose and free with these outlines and have fun with them. As you can see, I'm creating a ruffly outline on a smooth-edged leaf.

20 Outline the sunflower petals on the garden pail with Lemon Custard Outdoor Dimensional paint. Again, my painted sunflower petals have smooth edges, but I can create a special look by drawing wiggly lines on some of them.

21 On the rim of the pail, outline the bumblebee wings with Wicker White Outdoor Dimensional paint to lift them off the background and make them stand out.

22 On very small items like the wooden handles of the little trowel and cultivator, the fine point of the Outdoor Dimensional paint applicator makes it easy to paint tiny flowers. Start by painting a couple of clusters of one-stroke leaves with Thicket on a small flat brush. Draw some daisy petals using Wicker White and add centers with a dot of Lemon Custard.

The Outdoor paint has a sealer in it to withstand weather conditions. If added protection
is desired, I recommend using a spray lacquer
in your choice of finish.

pansy candles

*C*andles are a great gift idea and a pretty accessory for any room. Using the Enamels paints makes the designs last longer on a wax candle than using regular acrylic paints. Just make sure you use a candle that is not heavily scented, as the extra oils found in scented candles could affect the paint's adhesion. In this project, we will paint a short two-toned pillar candle and a frosted glass plate for it to sit on. You can also use the Enamels paints to create matching glass votives to put little tea candles in, or a stemmed glass goblet for a larger votive. The whole set would make a lovely addition to your dinner table for a candle-lit evening.

FolkArt Enamels Paints

 Thicket

 Lemon Custard

 School Bus Yellow

Fuchsia

 Violet Pansy

 Yellow Ochre

 Dioxazine Purple

Wicker White

Surface

- Two-color pillar candle
- Frosted glass plate
- Clear glass votives and goblet

Preparation

- Clean glass with a soft cloth and rubbing alcohol. Trace and transfer the patterns. (Patterns are shown on page 156.)

Brushes: FolkArt Enamel

- no. 6 flat
- no. 8 flat
- no. 12 flat
- no. 16 flat

Additional Supplies

- FolkArt Enamels Clear Medium

Pansy Candle

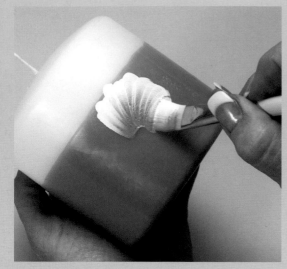

1 Double load a no. 16 flat with Wicker White and Yellow Ochre. Paint a shell stroke for the back petal, keeping the Wicker White to the outer edge.

2 Using the same loaded brush, pick up Violet Pansy and School Bus Yellow; paint the two side petals, keeping the purple to the outer edge.

3 Using the same brush and colors, flip the brush so the yellow side is to the outer edge and paint two more shell strokes.

4 Load the same brush with Dioxazine Purple and School Bus Yellow; paint two small teardrop petals to finish the pansy.

6 Use the handle end of the brush to place a dot of School Bus Yellow in the center.

5 Double load a no. 8 flat with Thicket and School Bus Yellow; paint the yellow centers with short chisel-edge strokes.

7 Double load a no. 16 flat with Fuchsia and Wicker White; paint the opening bud on the left side of the full pansy.

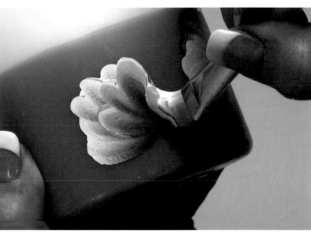

8 Pick up School Bus Yellow on the Wicker White side of the brush and paint smaller petals in the center front.

9 Add three small chisel-edge petals on the sides with the same brush and colors. Paint a mix of large and small leaves to fill in around the blossoms using Thicket and School Bus Yellow on a no. 16 flat.

10 The opening bud to the right of the full pansy is painted with Wicker White, Fuchsia and a little bit of School Bus Yellow. The smaller bud above it is Yellow Ochre.

Pansy Glass Plate

1 A frosted glass plate painted with a circlet of pansies makes a pretty stand for your pillar candle. Double load a no. 16 flat with Fuchsia and Wicker White. Start with the pink pansies and buds, using the same strokes as you did for the pansies on the pillar candle. Pick up School Bus Yellow on the brush for the side petals. Place the pink pansies as shown on the plate.

2 For the yellow pansies, load the no. 16 flat with Yellow Ochre, School Bus Yellow and Wicker White; paint them next to the pink pansies. Keep the Yellow Ochre to the outside edge of the petals.

hint

It's easier and keeps the colors consistent if you paint the buds at the same time as you paint the full pansy blossoms of each color.

3 Pick up Wicker White, School Bus Yellow and Violet Pansy; paint the light purple pansies and buds on the plate as shown. Keep the Violet Pansy to the outside edge of the petals.

4 Double load a no. 16 flat with Violet Pansy and School Bus Yellow; paint all the lower, teardrop petals on all the open pansies, keeping the purple edge of the brush to the outside. Double load a no. 8 flat with Thicket and School Bus Yellow and paint the chisel edge strokes in the centers, then dot in the centers with School Bus Yellow. Double load a no. 16 flat with Thicket and School Bus Yellow and pick up a touch of Wicker White. Paint the large and small leaves and pull the stems.

Pansy Glass Votives, Goblet and Plaid Design

plaid design

 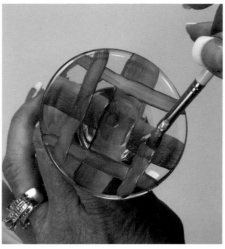 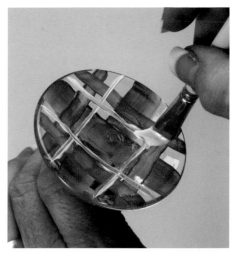

1 To add a coordinating plaid design to the underside of the base of the goblet shown below, load a no. 12 flat with a mix of Fuchsia and Wicker White and paint the widest stripes.

2 Load a no. 6 flat with a mix of Violet Pansy and Wicker White and paint the narrower stripes.

3 Load Lemon Custard onto the chisel edge of the brush and paint the thin yellow pinstripes.

hint

To thin the paint for the plaid design, load the brush into Clear Medium, then into your paint color. This keeps the paint more transparent-looking on glassware.

Using the same colors and brushes you used on the pillar candle and frosted glass candle plate, you can paint a garland of pansies around a clear glass goblet, and a single pansy blossom on small, clear glass votives. Choose glass with a smooth surface to make painting easier.

parrot tulips outdoor rug

Need a small rug for your front porch but can't find the right color or design? In this project I'll show you how to paint spectacular tulips on a vinyl rug that's just the right size for your front door. Remnants of vinyl flooring can be purchased at home improvement centers or flooring stores very inexpensively. It doesn't matter what the design on the front side of the flooring is because we're painting on the back side! So get the cheapest remnant you can find. If you want to paint a rug that's much larger than the one shown here, I suggest you basecoat the back side of the vinyl flooring with a latex interior house paint in an eggshell or satin finish, then use an exterior grade sealer when all the painting is done.

FolkArt Outdoor Opaque Paints

Light Blue

Wicker White

Thicket

Lemon Custard

Violet Pansy

Berry Wine

Surface

- Vinyl flooring remnant, approximately 2 feet (61cm) wide by 3 feet (91cm) long.

Preparation

- Clean the back side of the flooring remnant with a damp cloth to remove dust and dirt. Trace and transfer the pattern. (Pattern is shown on page 157.)

Brushes: One Stroke for acrylics

- no. 12 flat
- 1-inch (25mm) flat
- no. 2 script liner

Additional Supplies

- FolkArt Outdoor Flow Medium
- Scissors or craft knife
- One Stroke Faux Finish Sponge
- Exterior-grade, water-based varnish

Stems, Leaves and Pink Tulips

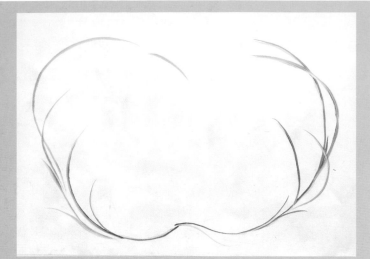

1 Cut the vinyl flooring several inches larger all around than your finished design will be to allow room for cutting the outside shape when the painting is done. Turn the vinyl piece over so the back side is up and basecoat with Wicker White paint. To make the faux sky background shown here, double load a moistened faux finishing sponge with Light Blue and Wicker White. Pick up a little Flow Medium to help move the paint. Use a circular motion to achieve the subtle mottled look. Let dry. Double load a 1-inch (25mm) flat with Thicket and Lemon Custard and staying up on the chisel edge, paint curving stems to establish the outside shape of the design.

2 Using the same brush and colors, paint the long tulip leaves on and around the stems. Push down on the bristles to get the wider parts of the leaves, then turn the brush and lift to the tip. A couple of the leaves at the bottom fold over on themselves—see page 50 for step-by-step instructions on painting folded tulip leaves.

3 Double load a 1-inch (25mm) flat with Berry Wine and Wicker White; add a touch of Lemon Custard to the Wicker White side. Paint the back petal, wiggling up to a point and keeping the lighter colors to the outside edge.

4 Reverse the direction of your bristles without lifting the brush, and wiggle back down to the base.

5 Add two side petals, still keeping the lighter side of the brush to the outside edges of the petals. Don't worry if these petals aren't perfect—the front petals will overlap them.

6 To paint the two shorter front petals, add a little bit more Wicker White to your brush to give a layering effect.

7 As tulips open up fully, their outside petals tend to bend and droop. Add a drooping petal by wiggling down one side, then turning and pulling smoothly back up.

8 To save time, paint all the tulips in the design that are this color before going on to the next color. Make some of the tulips very full, some not as full, and then add a bud or two. All of the stems will be added later.

Purple-and-Yellow Tulips

9 Double load a 1-inch (25mm) flat with Violet Pansy and Wicker White; add a touch of Lemon Custard to the Wicker White side. Paint the back petal first, wiggling up to a point and keeping the purple to the outside edge. Reverse the direction of your bristles without lifting the brush and wiggle back down to the base.

10 Paint the side petals by wiggling up to a point, then press down hard on the bristles as you slide down on the chisel to give a "turned-edge" effect to the petals.

11 Add more petals to the sides and front by making them shorter than the back petals to give a layered effect.

12 Paint the drooping petals on the sides, flipping the brush over so the lighter colors are on the outside. Wiggle out to the tip, reverse direction, stay up on the chisel and slide back to the base.

13 Add as many drooping petals as you like, but keep the lighter colors to the outside on all of them. Some of these contrasting-colored petals can be added facing upward too.

14 Place more of the purple-and-yellow tulips around the design, facing in different directions and following the curves of the leaves. Add partially open buds wherever the design seems to need them.

Calyxes, Stems and Leaves

15 Double load a 1-inch (25mm) flat with Thicket and Lemon Custard. At the base of the tulip, touch, lean away from the flower, and pull short strokes, grabbing the base of the flower each time you stroke.

16 Continue pulling the last stroke downward to form the stem. It's easier to paint all the bases and stems at one time since your brush is loaded with the right colors.

17 If needed, go back in and re-establish some of the leaves, cleaning them up and extending a few of the tips.

Hummingbird

1 To paint the hummingbird, double load a no. 12 flat with Thicket and Wicker White and paint a half circle for the head, keeping the green to the outside.

2 Paint a long one-stroke leaf downward to shape the bird's back.

3 Double load a no. 12 flat with Berry Wine and Wicker White; paint a small teardrop stroke to form the cheek.

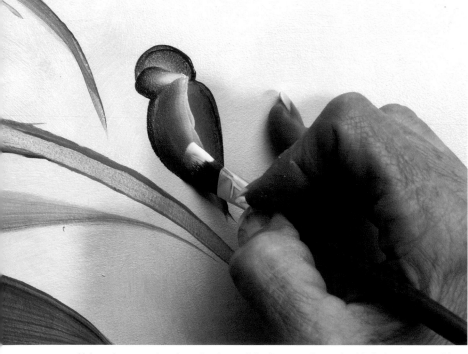

5 Double load the no. 12 flat with Thicket and Wicker White; paint the back wing by painting a one-stroke leaf shape for the shoulder.

4 Using the same brush and colors, slide down to form the bird's breast, watching the outer edge to draw the shape and keeping the Berry Wine to the outside edge.

Feathers, Eye and Beak

6 Pull short chisel-edge strokes for the feathers. Start at the outside tip of each feather, lead with the white side of the brush and pull inward toward the white edge of the wing. Stroke the feathers close enough so they touch each other.

7 Finish pulling the feathers on the back wing before starting the front wing. The front wing is painted using the same procedure as the back wing.

8 For the front wing's feathers, pull short, chisel-edge strokes in toward the wing's base, leading with the white side of the brush, and joining the white of the feathers with the white of the wing base.

10 Load a no. 2 script liner with inky Thicket. Draw the beak outward from the face, and dot in the eye. Highlight the eye and the base of the beak with Wicker White on the tip of the script liner.

9 Using the same brush and colors, pull tail feathers in toward the lower end of the bird's body, leading with the white side of the brush. Place the longest feather in the middle and gradually shorter ones on each side.

Cutting Outside Edge to Shape

1 Check your finished design to make sure you like it, and then let all the paint dry completely.

2 To shape the rug, use a sharp pair of scissors or a craft knife to cut around the outside of the design. If you wish, paint the cut edges with colors to match the leaves and tulips.

If you will be using your rug outdoors or where it will get a lot of foot traffic, seal and protect the rug with two to three coats of an exterior grade, water-based varnish, letting it dry between coats.

painted knobs and pulls

*H*ere are twelve easy and fun designs to paint on drawer pulls, cabinet knobs and door knobs. If you are new to One-Stroke painting, practice the strokes with larger brushes until you are comfortable before attempting them with the smaller brushes required for these knobs and pulls. When using brushes that are smaller than a no. 12 flat, load the brush completely with the lighter color and then sideload to pick up the darker color. After the brush is fully loaded, continue to sideload the lighter color every time to keep the light color crisp. To protect your painted door knobs and cabinet pulls from wear and tear, use two to three coats of a clear spray lacquer, letting dry between coats.

FolkArt Acrylics, Artists' Pigments and Enamels Paints

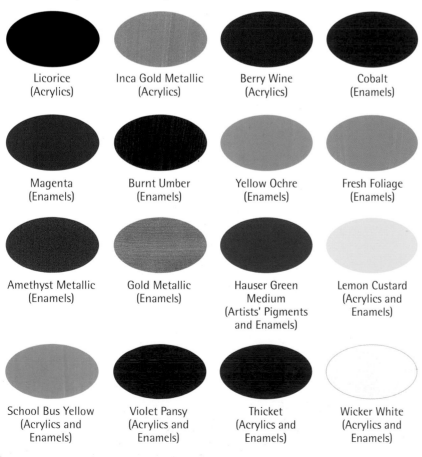

| Licorice (Acrylics) | Inca Gold Metallic (Acrylics) | Berry Wine (Acrylics) | Cobalt (Enamels) |

| Magenta (Enamels) | Burnt Umber (Enamels) | Yellow Ochre (Enamels) | Fresh Foliage (Enamels) |

| Amethyst Metallic (Enamels) | Gold Metallic (Enamels) | Hauser Green Medium (Artists' Pigments and Enamels) | Lemon Custard (Acrylics and Enamels) |

| School Bus Yellow (Acrylics and Enamels) | Violet Pansy (Acrylics and Enamels) | Thicket (Acrylics and Enamels) | Wicker White (Acrylics and Enamels) |

Surfaces
- A variety of door knobs, cabinet knobs and drawer pulls in wood, metal, glass, ceramic, brass, pewter and porcelain. All are available at home improvement centers.

Preparation
- Clean glass knobs with rubbing alcohol. Sand and seal wooden knobs.

Brushes: One Stroke for acrylics
- nos. 2, 6 and 8 flats
- no. 2 script liner

Brushes: One Stroke Enamel
- nos. 2 and 6 flats
- nos. 1 and 2 script liners
- 1/4-inch (6mm) scruffy
- 1/8-inch (3mm) scruffy

Additional Supplies
- Pencil
- Cotton swab
- FolkArt Enamels Clear Medium
- Spray lacquer in matte, satin or gloss finish

Five-petal Flowers and Comma Strokes

comma strokes

  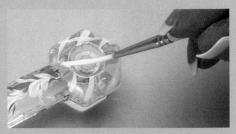

1 Using Enamels paints, load a no. 2 script liner with Wicker White and then side load Gold Metallic. Paint a few sets of double comma strokes on the handle of a glass drawer pull. Lead with Gold Metallic for some of the strokes and Wicker White for others.

2 Using the same brush, pick up more Gold Metallic and add a few more scrolls and comma strokes.

3 Load a no. 2 script liner with Wicker White and thin to an inky consistency with Clear Medium. Paint cross-hatching on the two knob ends of the pull.

five-petal flowers

1 Using Enamels paints, load a no. 6 flat brush into Clear Medium then sideload with Wicker White. Paint a cluster of five-petal flowers in the center of a glass door knob..

2 Using the same brush and color, add tiny leaves around the outside of the flower cluster. Switch to a no. 1 script liner and add tiny comma strokes to fill in any empty areas.

3 Dot in the flower centers with a no. 2 script liner, using lots of Wicker White paint to create raised dots.

comma strokes

1 Double load a no. 6 flat with Cobalt and Wicker White Enamels. Begin painting sets of double comma strokes around the rim of a smooth porcelain door knob, alternating the direction in which each set is facing.

2 Complete the circle of comma strokes, spacing them out evenly around the rim of the knob.

3 Pick up a little more Wicker White on your brush and re-stroke some of the commas to highlight and fill in.

iris

1 All the knobs are this page are ceramic, so use Enamels paints. Load a no. 2 script liner with Violet Pansy and add a touch of Wicker White. The two upper petals are pressure-and-lift strokes. The two bottom petals are painted like tiny one-stroke leaves.

2 To paint the center petal, load a no. 2 script liner with School Bus Yellow and sideload into Magenta. Stroke the petal the same as you would a one-stroke leaf.

3 Load a no. 2 script liner with Lemon Custard and sideload with Thicket. Pull a stem downward. Load a no. 2 flat with the same colors and pull little iris leaves starting at the base and stroking up to the tips.

daisy face

1 Using Enamels paints, double load a no. 6 flat brush with Magenta and Wicker White; paint a circle of daisy petals.

2 Load a small scruffy with School Bus Yellow and Lemon Custard; add a touch of Hauser Green Medium. Pounce the center of the flower. Let dry. With Wicker White and a bit of Magenta, pounce the pink cheeks.

3 Load a no. 2 script liner with inky Burnt Umber; paint the facial features. To finish, use a toothpick or a pencil with Wicker White to place tiny dots around the center.

ferns

1 Using Enamels paints, load a no. 2 script liner with Thicket; paint the fern spine.

2 Load a no. 1 script liner with Thicket and add a touch of Lemon Custard. Paint fern leaves along one side of the stem, pulling each leaf inward toward the spine.

3 Finish with the fern leaves on the other side of the spine.

Palm Tree, Grapes and Dot Flowers

palm tree

1 Use Enamels paints for this brass knob. Load a no. 2 script liner with Burnt Umber and Yellow Ochre; paint the trunk of the palm tree with little push-lift strokes, getting narrower at the top.

2 Load a no. 2 script liner with Thicket; paint the first layer of palm fronds.

3 Pick up Fresh Foliage on the brush and stroke in lighter palm fronds to highlight. If the palm fronds get too light, add a touch more Thicket to re-establish some of the darker fronds.

grapes

1 This ceramic knob is trimmed with metal and would be perfect for a kitchen cabinet door. Using Enamels, double load a no. 6 flat with Fresh Foliage and Thicket. Paint the grape leaf and the one-stroke leaf.

2 Dampen a cotton swab with Clear Medium; squeeze out the excess. Load it with Amethyst Metallic and then add a touch of Violet Pansy. Touch the swab onto the knob lightly and spin the swab with your fingers to make each grape.

3 Add tiny curlicues with a no. 2 script liner loaded with inky Thicket.

dot flowers

1 This knob is pewter so use Enamels paints. Place light pencil lines for your vertical stripes and the horizontal leaf band. Load a no. 6 flat with Magenta; add a touch of Wicker White to soften. Paint vertical stripes on the lower half.

2 Load a no. 6 flat with Wicker White and Fresh Foliage; paint a horizontal band of leaves across the top edge of the stripes. Outline the bottom edge of each leaf and pull stems into the centers with Wicker White on a no. 2 script liner.

3 Load a no. 1 script liner with Amethyst Metallic; paint the flowers by dotting in little circles. The centers are dots of Lemon Custard.

Butterflies, Scrollwork and Roses

butterflies

1 Using acrylic paints, basecoat a plain wooden knob with two coats of Licorice. Let dry. Double load a no. 6 flat with Hauser Green Medium and Wicker White. Paint the fern by pulling little chisel-edge strokes downward toward the center.

2 Double load a no. 8 flat with Berry Wine and Wicker White; paint the open rose-buds. Double load a no. 8 flat with Thicket and Wicker White and paint the leaves.

3 Load a no. 2 flat with Wicker White; paint the butterfly wings. Use Hauser Green Medium for the bodies. Load a no. 2 flat with Lemon Custard and Wicker White; paint the five-petal flowers. Dot the centers with School Bus Yellow.

scrollwork

1 Using acrylics, basecoat a plain wooden knob with Licorice. Two coats may be needed for even coverage. Load a no. 2 script liner with Inca Gold Metallic. Paint loops around the edge of the knob and the base as shown.

2 Using the same brush and color, add cross-hatching inside the loops. Paint overlapping loops on the base.

3 Finish with sets of two and three comma strokes between the cross-hatched loops on the knob, and then add a dot where the comma strokes connect. On the base, add a dot to the top of each loop using a no. 1 script liner.

roses

1 Using acrylics, basecoat a wooden knob with two coats of Licorice. Let dry. Double load a no. 8 flat with Berry Wine and Wicker White; paint the rose. (See pages 40-41 for complete instructions on painting a cabbage rose.)

2 Double load a no. 8 flat with Hauser Green Medium and Wicker White; add a touch of Thicket to the Hauser Green Medium. Paint the larger leaves, then switch to a no. 2 flat for the smaller, one-stroke leaves.

3 Load a no. 6 flat with Wicker White and tap in some white filler flowers. Add Violet Pansy to the brush and tap in the purple filler flowers.

trompe l'oeil wall mural

*P*ainting on a wall can be a little scary the first time you try it. You're
worried that you may ruin the wall. But let me tell you, once you get
started painting on walls, you're not going to want to paint just on smaller
surfaces anymore. A wall is just a large surface that begs to be decorated.
If you are still unsure, then take a couple of pieces of poster board and
basecoat them the color of your wall. Let them dry and then tape them to
the wall using painter's tape. Paint your design on the poster board to see if
you are going to like it. Leave it up for a couple of days and then when you
are ready, take it down and paint the design directly on the wall. You'll be
a pro in no time!

FolkArt Acrylic Paints

| Wicker White | Sunflower | Butter Pecan | Thicket |

Surface

- Interior wall with smooth surface, base-coated with a satin or eggshell latex paint in white, available at any home improvement center or paint store.

Preparation

- Clean wall with a damp cloth. Let dry. Make sure there are no holes or bumps on the wall.

Brushes: One Stroke for acrylics

- no. 16 flat
- 1-inch (25mm) flat
- large scruffy
- no. 2 script liner

Additional Supplies

- FolkArt Glazing Medium
- FolkArt Floating Medium
- One Stroke Faux Finish Sponge
- Blue painter's tape
- Yard stick (meter stick)
- Level

Faux Finish Background and Wall Sconce

1 Before painting the trompe l'oeil sconce and greenery, begin with a very subtle faux finish on the wall in a coordinating color of pale yellow and white. After dampening a round faux finishing sponge with clean water, rub the sponge in some glazing medium, then work in some Wicker White and a touch of Sunflower.

2 To avoid painting the faux finish where the sconce will be, you can tape a piece of tracing paper to the wall in the shape of the sconce. Using a circular motion, apply the faux finish to the wall and let it dry completely.

3 Load a 1-inch (25mm) flat with floating medium, then sideload with Butter Pecan. Starting on the outer edge, paint the shape of the sconce, working from top to bottom toward the center. Then paint each rib. Be sure to keep the Butter Pecan side of the brush to the right on the right side of the sconce, and to the left on the left side of the sconce. Watch the Butter Pecan side of your brush as you draw each rib.

4 To give the trompe l'oeil effect of a three-dimensional shape, load a 1-inch (25mm) flat with Floating Medium and then sideload with Butter Pecan. Turn the brush so the Butter Pecan side is against the outer edge of the sconce; add shading along this edge all the way to the bottom. Reload the brush with floating medium and Butter Pecan and shade along the other side of the sconce, turning the brush so the Butter Pecan is next to the edge of the sconce. Shade all the way to the bottom.

Moss and Ferns

5 Double load a large scruffy with Wicker White and Thicket, and add a touch of Sunflower on the Wicker White side. Pounce moss all along the top of the sconce, tapering off in a few places where the moss hangs down the side.

6 Double load a 1-inch (25mm) flat with Thicket and Wicker White; add a touch of Sunflower to the Wicker White side. Pull the spines for the fern fronds out from the top of the mossy area, staying up on the chisel edge of the brush.

7 Using the same brush and colors, pull the broadleaf fern leaves in toward the spine, occasionally pick-ing up floating medium to keep the paint smooth. Lift to the chisel just before you reach the spine—this helps create a light and airy look to the fern fronds.

8 The lacy-leafed ferns are painted using the same colors loaded on a no. 16 flat. Lead with the darker color and stay up on the chisel edge. Layer the fern frond with some lighter and some darker leaves.

Ferns, Ivy and Shadow Leaves

10 Painting three varieties of fern makes this arrangement more lush and interesting. You can also add little details such as the unfurling fronds shown here.

9 Double load a 1-inch (25mm) flat with Thicket and Wicker White and add a touch of Sunflower on the white side; paint the ferns with the pointed tips. Start at the spine and push down, then lift to the point, pulling outward from the spine.

11 To paint the ivy leaves, double load a 1-inch (25mm) flat with Thicket and Wicker White. Pick up Sunflower occasionally on your brush to vary the leaf colors. As the leaves get smaller, you can switch to a no. 16 flat to paint the baby ivy leaves.

12 Load a no. 16 flat with floating medium, add a touch of Thicket to the chisel edge and blend well. Paint transparent shadow leaves here and there to add depth to the greenery. Paint a few curlicues using the no. 2 script liner loaded with Thicket.

13 Step back from your work and see if there's anything you need to change or add, but resist the temptation to overdo it. The arrangement looks more natural if it is slightly imperfect looking. After all, nature is not perfect.

14 Below the sconce at chair rail height is a border of ferns—the same kinds of ferns that are in the sconce. Using blue painter's tape, mask off a 1-inch (25mm) wide band both above and below the border. Use a level to make the lines straight. Paint these upper and lower bands with Butter Pecan. Remove the painter's tape before the paint is completely dry. Paint the spines for the ferns first to map out their location. Paint the fern varieties the same as you did in Steps 6 through 9, using the same brushes and colors.

15 Allow the ferns to overlap the top and bottom Butter Pecan bands in a few places for a more graceful look, and add details like unfurling fronds, an occasional loose leaf, and some curlicues.

16 In the wall area below the chair rail border, add sprigs of fern fronds randomly here and there. Make some of them shorter with a few leaves and some longer, and let them face in different directions. Use the same colors and brushes you used to paint the ferns in the border. Fill in with a few one-stroke leaves in sets of three on a short stem.

patterns

All patterns on pages 152-157 may be hand-traced or photocopied for personal use only. The percentage of enlargement needed to bring each pattern up to full size is shown next to the pattern.

project 1: wildflowers mailbox
Enlarge at 200%

project 2: personal care set
Enlarge at 250%

project 3: wild rose cigar box purse
Enlarge at 222%

project 4: daisy flowerpots

PINK DAISIES
Enlarge at 154%

YELLOW DAISIES
Enlarge at 182%

WHITE DAISIES
Enlarge at 182%

project 5: fruit & plaid tile tray

APPLE
Enlarge at 222%

BLUEBERRIES
Enlarge at 222%

PEAR
Enlarge at 222%

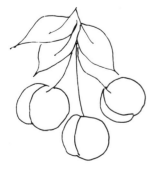

CHERRIES
Enlarge at 222%

PLUM
Enlarge at 222%

BLACKBERRIES
Enlarge at 222%

project 6: wildflowers wall cabinet
Enlarge at 200%

project 7: cabbage rose glass plate
Enlarge at 182%

project 8: sunflower garden tools

WATERING CAN
Enlarge at 333%

GARDEN PAIL
Enlarge at 333%

project 9: pansy candles

PILLAR CANDLE
Enlarge at 105%

GLASS PLATE
Enlarge at 118%

project 10: parrot tulips outdoor rug
Enlarge at 200%, and then again at 182%

Resources

U.S. RETAILERS

folkart paints & mediums; one-stroke brushes:

Plaid Enterprises, Inc.
3225 Westech Dr.
Norcross, GA 30092-3500
USA
Phone: 800-842-4197
www.plaidonline.com

Dewberry Designs, Inc.
365 Citrus Tower Blvd.
Clermont, FL 34711
Phone: 352-394-7344
www.onestroke.com

CANADIAN RETAILERS

Crafts Canada
120 North Archibald St.
Thunder Bay, ON P7C 3X8
888-482-5978
www.craftscanada.ca

Folk Art Enterprises
P.O. Box 1088
Ridgetown, ON, N0P 2C0
Tel: 800-265-9434

MacPherson Arts & Crafts
91 Queen St. E.
P.O. Box 1810
St. Mary's, ON, N4X 1C2
Tel: 800-238-6663
www.macphersoncrafts.com

Maureen McNaughton Enterprises
RR #2
Belwood, ON, N0B 1J0
Tel: 519-843-5648
www.maureenmcnaughton.com

U.K. RETAILERS

Atlantis Art Materials
7-9 Plumber's Row
London E1 1EQ
020 7377 8855
www.atlantisart.co.uk

Crafts World (head office)
No. 8 North Street
Guildford
Surrey GU1 4 AF
07000 757070

Green & Stone
259 Kings Road
London SW3 5EL
020 7352 0837
www.greenandstone.com

Help Desk
HobbyCraft Superstore
The Peel Centre
St. Ann Way
Gloucester
Gloucestershire GL1 5SF
01452 424999
www.hobbycraft.co.uk

The best in decorative painting instruction and inspiration is from North Light Books!

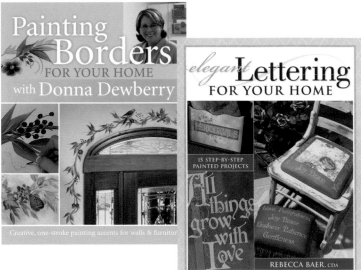

Fantastic Floorcloths You Can Paint in a Day

Want to refresh your home décor without the time and expense of extensive redecorating? Then painting canvas floorcloths is for you! Choose from 23 projects simple enough to create in a few hours. Popular decorative painters Judy Diephouse and Lynne Deptula show you step by step how to paint designs ranging from florals to graphic patterns to holiday motifs, including some especially appropriate for kids' rooms. 12 accessory ideas inspire you to create a coordinated look. *Fantastic Floorcloths You Can Paint in a Day* makes adding creative touches to the home as easy as picking up a paintbrush.
ISBN-13: 978-1-58180-603-8
ISBN-10: 1-58180-603-5 • Paperback, 128 pages, #33161

Flowers A to Z with Donna Dewberry

Painting your favorite flowers is easy and fun with Donna Dewberry's popular one-stroke technique! You'll see how to paint more than 50 garden flowers and wildflowers in an array of stunning colors. Discover Donna's secrets for painting leaves, vines, foliage, flower petals, blossoms, and floral bouquets. Add beauty and elegance to any project including furniture, walls, pottery, birdbaths and more!
ISBN-13: 978-1-58180-484-3
ISBN-10: 1-58180-484-9 • Paperback, 144 pages, #32803

Painting Borders for Your Home with Donna Dewberry

Donna shows you how to use her renowned one-stroke method to create colorful borders that give character and style to every room in your home. Coordinating borders accompany each project, so you can make perfect accessories. With photos showing the borders in actual homes, you'll find the inspiration you need to create masterpieces for walls and furniture throughout your house.
ISBN-13: 978-1-58180-600-7
ISBN-10: 1-58180-600-0 • Paperback, 128 pages, #33125

Elegant Lettering for Your Home

Here's everything you need to create beautiful lettering designs to enhance any room! Inside you'll find 12 gorgeous, step-by-step projects featuring lettering on home accessories, furniture and walls. Plus, you'll learn a wide range of tips and techniques, ranging from adjusting lettering fonts to arranging design elements and embellishments for the most pleasing effect.
ISBN-13: 978-1-58180-578-9
ISBN-10: 1-58180-578-0 • Paperback, 128 pages, #33041

These books and other fine North Light titles are available at your local arts & crafts retailer, bookstore, or from online suppliers.